Quick Scales & Modes

Simple Search

No-Fuss, Flick-thru Guides

Jake Jackson

Publisher and Creative Director: Nick Wells

Project, design and media integration: Jake Jackson

Website and software: David Neville with Stevens Dumpala and Steve Moulton

Editorial: Gillian Whitaker

First published 2022 by
FLAME TREE PUBLISHING
6 Melbray Mews
Fulham, London SW6 3NS
United Kingdom
flametreepublishing.com

Music information site:
flametreemusic.com

26 25 24 23 22
10 9 8 7 6 5 4 3 2 1

ISBN: 978-1-83964-946-2

Printed and bound in the UK by Clays Ltd, Elcograf S.p.A.

The CIP record for this book is available from the British Library.

Jake Jackson is a writer and musician. He has created and contributed to over 20 practical music books, including *Reading Music Made Easy*, *Play Flamenco* and *Piano and Keyboard Chords*. His music is available on iTunes, Amazon and Spotify amongst others.

Alan Brown (Notation). A former member of the Scottish National Orchestra, Alan now works as a freelance musician, with several leading UK orchestras, and as a consultant in music and IT. Alan has had several compositions published, developed a set of music theory CD-Roms, co-written a series of Bass Guitar Examination Handbooks and worked on over 100 further titles.

See & Hear
Web Links

Melodies
& Solos

Quick Scales & Modes

Simple Search

No-Fuss, Flick-thru Guides

Jake Jackson

Flame Tree
Music
CHORDS • SCALES
flametreemusic.com

Contents

Online access · flametreemusic.com · Scan the code to hear the chord

The Scales & Modes

Online access
flametreemusic.com

Scan the code
to hear the chord

How to Use This Book

This useful new book will provide musicians of all levels with a solid point of reference that can be used to enhance music-making of all kinds.

The Anatomy of a Scale

Scales are invariably named after their **starting note** or **tonic**, also known as the **key note**, e.g. C in a **C Major** scale. It is common to number notes of a scale, with the tonic counting as one, so that we can refer to, for example, 'the fifth degree of the scale' or simply 'the fifth'. Depending on the range of your instrument, you are quite likely to be able to play higher or lower than the one-octave scales given in this book.

Scale Pattern Key

For each of the scales and modes included in this book their scale pattern is included. This shows the relationship between each note in the scale. For example, the scale pattern of the **major scale** (also known as the **Ionian mode**) is:

T T S T T T S

S = semitone (half step); **T** = tone (whole step)

Also used in some scales:

m3 = minor third (three semitones)
a2 = augmented second (also three semitones).

Online access
flametreemusic.com

**Scan the code
to hear the chord**

6

Modes

Most scales can be used as the basis of further scales with different interval structures, starting the new scale on each degree of the old scale. The main example is the set of major scale modes, which appear in several groups.

- **Dorian**: contains the notes of the major scale starting from its **second** degree.

- **Phrygian**: contains the notes of the major scale starting from its **third** degree.

- **Lydian**: contains the notes of the major scale starting from its **fourth** degree.

- **Mixolydian**: contains the notes of the major scale starting from its **fifth** degree.

- **Aeolian**: contains the notes of the major scale starting from its **sixth** degree.

- **Locrian**: contains the notes of the major scale starting from its **seventh** degree.

Even though the major scale and its modal scales use the same notes, because they have different **key notes** they do not have the same tonality. For example, while the major scale has a major third interval from the root to the third note and a major seventh interval from the root to the seventh note, in contrast, the Dorian modal scale has a flattened third interval from the root to the third note and a flattened seventh interval from the root to the seventh note, making it a type of minor scale.

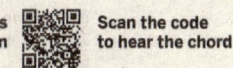

Online access
flametreemusic.com

Scan the code
to hear the chord

Scale and Mode Groups

This book contains 20 of the most useful scales and modes, for each of the 12 chromatic tones. The scales and modes are divided into four groups (Major, Minor, Dominant and Unusual).

The Major Group

The third degree is important in giving a scale its basic flavour and all scales in this group have a third (four semitones, e.g. C to E) and usually a major seventh (11 semitones, e.g. C to B). Some other scales with major thirds also have minor sevenths (10 semitones, e.g. C to B♭) and appear in the Dominant Group.

- **Major**: the most commonly used scale in western music, being the 'Doh, Re, Mi' scale used in *The Sound Of Music*.
  Scale Pattern: T T S T T T S

- **Major Pentatonic**: this is a major scale with gaps (no fourth or seventh) and can be heard in many traditional tunes from places as far apart as Scotland and China.
  Scale Pattern: T T m3 T m3

- **Lydian Mode:** similar to a major scale except for the raised fourth degree.
  Scale Pattern: T T T S T T S

- **Lydian Augmented**: this is a modal version of the melodic minor (starting on its parent scale's third step) and is essentially a lydian with a raised, or augmented, fifth. It is often used in modern jazz.
  Scale Pattern: T T T T S T S

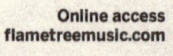

Online access
flametreemusic.com

Scan the code
to hear the chord

The Minor Group

Scales in this group feature minor thirds, and include standard minor, and several modal scales.

- **Natural Minor (Aeolian Mode):** based on a major scale but starts on its sixth degree. Many folk and traditional tunes use this scale; significant notes are the flat six and a seventh.
  Scale Pattern: T S T T S T T

- **Harmonic Minor**: this is identical to the natural minor except for the seventh degree, which is a semitone higher to make a major dominant chord possible, essential for most progressions in minor keys.
  Scale Pattern: T S T T S a2 S

- **Melodic Minor**: traditionally played with major sixth and seventh on the way up and lowered sixth and seventh on the way down. Improvising players often abandon the descending version and use exclusively the ascending form, which is consequently also called the **Jazz Melodic Minor**.
  Scale Pattern: T S T T T T S (ascending form)

- **Dorian Mode**: another important modal scale, also heard in jazz but in many folk songs too. Notice that it has a major sixth but a minor seventh.
  Scale Pattern: T S T T T S T

- **Minor Pentatonic**: another variant, which can be thought of as a simplified minor scale with gaps. Like the major pentatonic, it is often found in folk melodies and rock solos.
  Scale Pattern: m3 T T m3 T

- **Blues**: created by adding one chromatic note (a raised fourth or a flattened fifth) to the minor pentatonic scale. The blues scale can also be played over a dominant seventh chord.
Scale Pattern: m3 T S S m3 T

- **Phrygian Mode**: this is another scale sometimes heard in jazz or folk music. It is identical to the aeolian/natural minor except for its lowered second step.
Scale Pattern: S T T T S T T

- **Locrian Mode**: takes the notes of the phrygian and lowers its fifth step to give an unstable brooding quality.
Scale Pattern: S T T S T T T

- **Half Diminished**: raise the second degree of the locrian to create this scale, which is also a mode of the melodic minor.
Scale Pattern: T S T S T T T

Dominant Group

The essential characteristics of these scales are the major third and minor (lowered) seventh.

- **Mixolydian Mode**: a major scale starting on its fifth degree. You can also think of it as a major scale with a flattened seventh. Used in blues, rock, jazz and folk music.
Scale Pattern: T T S T T S T

- **Phrygian Major/Spanish**: starts on the fifth degree of the harmonic minor scale with lowered second and seventh notes. Works well over a dominant chord with a flattened ninth. Commonly used in flamenco and heavy metal music.
Scale Pattern: S a2 S T S T T

- **Lydian Dominant:** this is a mode of the melodic minor and has the sharp fourth of a lydian and the flat seventh of a mixolydian. Used mainly in jazz.
Scale Pattern: T T T S T S T

- **Diminished/Octatonic:** this is created by adding the two altered ninths from the previous scale to the lydian dominant. It has nine different notes and can only be transposed a couple of times before it starts to repeat the same notes. Used mainly in jazz.
Scale Pattern: S T S T S T S T

A Few Unusual Scales

Most of these are used less often than most of the earlier scales and modes but are useful when exploring more experimental sounds.

- **Chromatic**: this can be used in conjunction with any chord. As it contains all twelve semitones it can't be transposed or turned into a mode without remaining uniquely itself.

- **Wholetone**: this also defies much transposition: if you took out every alternate note of the chromatic it would make one of the wholetone scales, the notes left making up the other. It will fit a dominant chord but with a little modification can give rise to a further set of modes.
Scale Pattern: T T T T T T

- **Neapolitan**: a wholetone scale that starts and finishes with a semitone; it is also a melodic minor with a flattened second. Used mainly in jazz and experimental music.
Scale Pattern: S T T T T T S

The Audio Links

Requirements: a camera and internet-ready smartphone (e.g. iPhone, any Android phone (e.g. Samsung Galaxy), Nokia Lumia, or camera-enabled tablet such as the iPad Mini). The best result is achieved using a Wi-Fi connection.

Either:

1. Point your camera at the QR code. Most modern smartphones read the link automatically and offer you the website **flametreemusic.com** to connect online.

Or:

1. Download any **free QR code reader**. An app store search will reveal a great many of these, so obviously it's best to go with the ones with the highest ratings and don't be afraid to try a few before you settle on the one that works best for you. Tapmedia's QR Code Reader app, Kaspersky QR Scanner or QR Code Reader by Scan are perfectly fine, although some of the free apps also have ads.

2. On your smartphone, open the app and **scan** the **QR code** at the base of any particular page.

Online access
flametreemusic.com

Scan the code
to hear the chord

Then:

3. Scanning the chord will bring you to the chord page. From there you can access and **hear** the complete library of scales and chords on **flametreemusic.com**.

    On pages where QR codes feature alongside particular chords and scales, those codes will take you directly to the relevant chord or scale on the website.

4. Use the drop-down menu to choose from **20 scales** or 12 **free chords** (50 with subscription) per key.

5. Click the sounds! Both piano and guitar audio is provided. This is particularly helpful when you're playing with others.

    The QR codes give you direct access to chords and scales. You can access a much wider range of chords if you register.

Online access
flametreemusic.com

Scan the code
to hear the chord

Easy Access

Organized from A to G keys

•

Each key gives 20 different scales
and modes

•

Flick through to find what you need

•

Check the notes under each diagram

•

Use the QR code to hear scales and chords

•

Online access
flametreemusic.com

Scan the code
to hear the chord

Quick Scales & Modes

Simple Search

No-Fuss, Flick-thru Guides

Online access
flametreemusic.com

Scan the code
to hear the chord

A
Major (Ionian Mode)

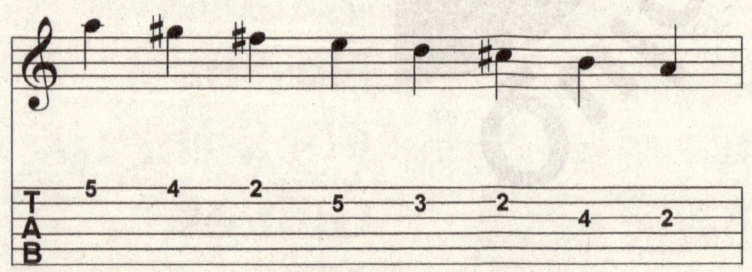

| **Scale pattern** | A B C# D E F# G# A |
| | A G# F# E D C# B A |

Online access
flametreemusic.com

Scan the code
to hear the chord

A
Major Pentatonic

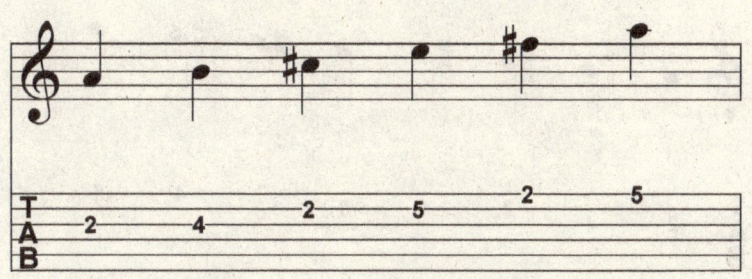

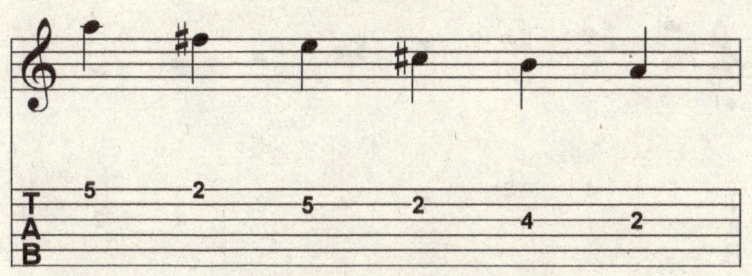

| **Scale pattern** | A B C# E F# A |
| | A F# E C# B A |

Online access
flametreemusic.com

Scan the code
to hear the chord

A
Lydian Mode

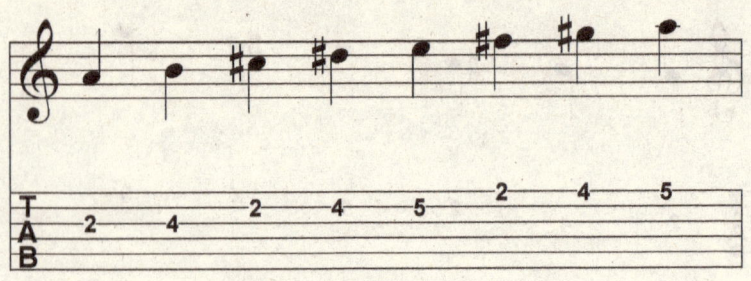

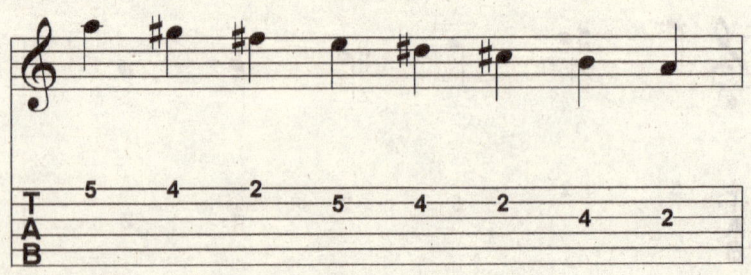

Scale pattern	A B C# D# E F# G# A
	A G# F# E D# C# B A

A
Lydian Augmented

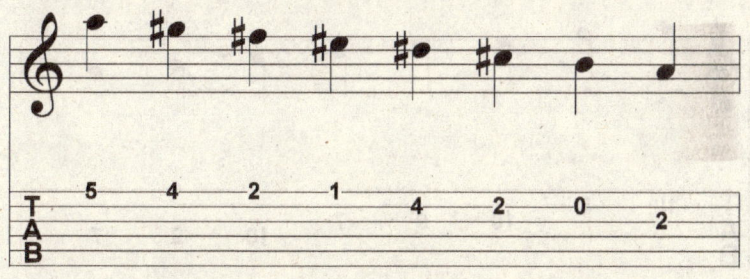

Scale pattern	A B C# D# E# F# G# A
	A G# F# E# D# C# B A

Online access
flametreemusic.com

Scan the code
to hear the chord

A
Natural Minor (Aeolian Mode)

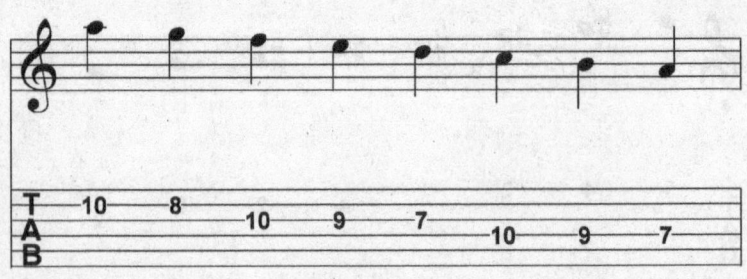

| **Scale pattern** | A B C D E F G A |
| | A G F E D C B A |

A
Harmonic Minor

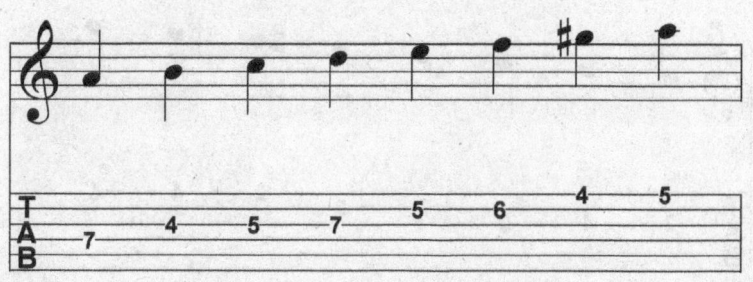

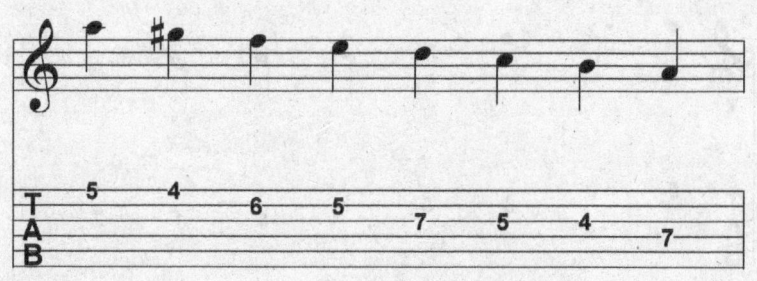

Scale pattern	A B C D E F G# A
	A G# F E D C B A

A
Melodic Minor

| **Scale pattern** | A B C D E F♯ G♯ A |
| | A G♮ F♮ E D C B A |

Online access
flametreemusic.com

Scan the code
to hear the chord

A
Dorian Mode

Scale pattern	A B C D E F# G A A G F# E D C B A

A
Minor Pentatonic

Scale pattern	ACDEGA
	AGEDCA

A
Blues

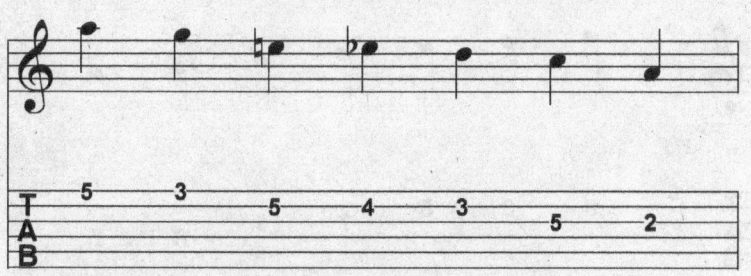

Scale pattern	A C D E♭ E♮ G A
	A G E♮ E♭ D C A

A
Phrygian Mode

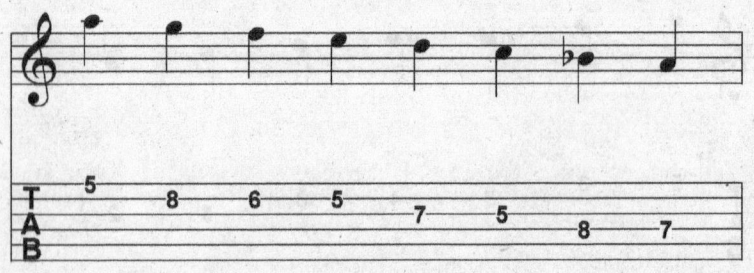

Scale pattern	A B♭ C D E F G A
	A G F E D C B♭ A

Online access
flametreemusic.com

Scan the code
to hear the chord

A
Locrian Mode

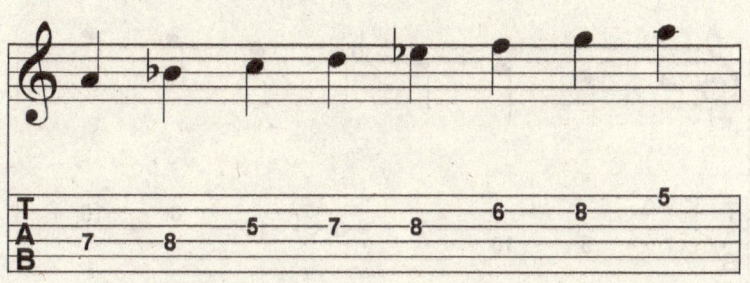

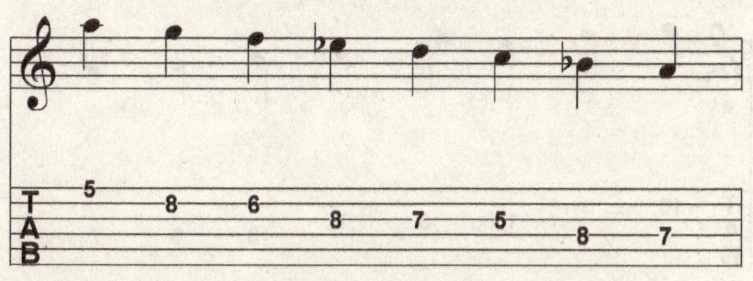

Scale pattern	A B♭ C D E♭ F G A
	A G F E♭ D C B♭ A

Online access
flametreemusic.com

Scan the code
to hear the chord

A
Half-diminished

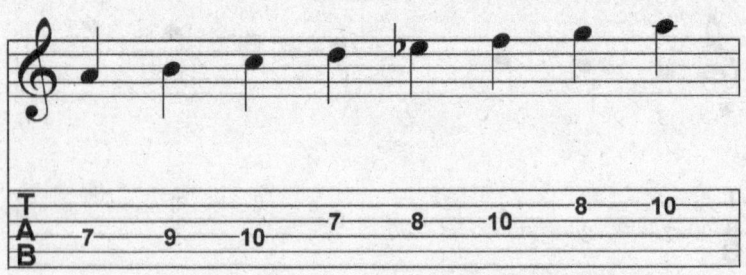

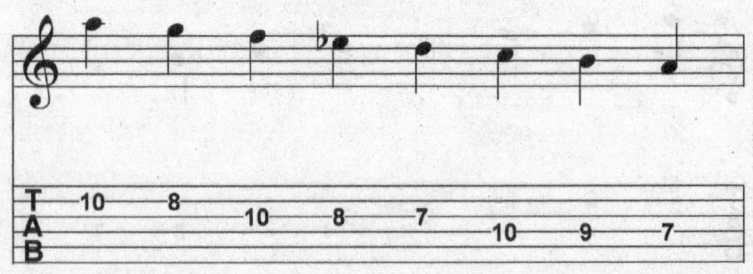

Scale pattern	A B C D E♭ F G A
	A G F E♭ D C B A

A
Myxolydian Mode

Scale pattern	A B C♯ D E F♯ G A
	A G F♯ E D C♯ B A

A
Phrygian Major/Spanish

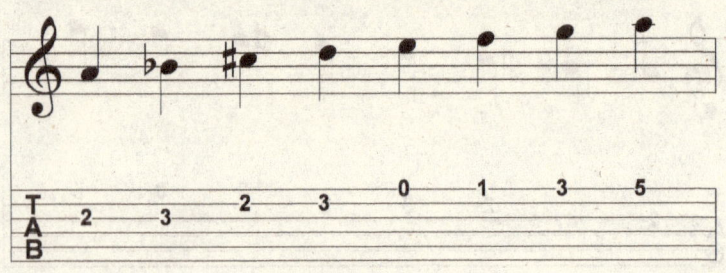

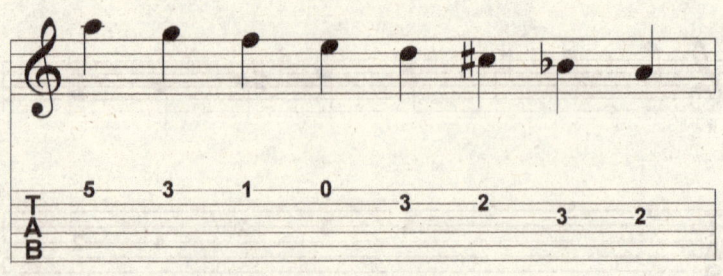

Scale pattern	A B♭ C♯ D E F G A
	A G F E D C♯ B♭ A

A
Lydian Dominant

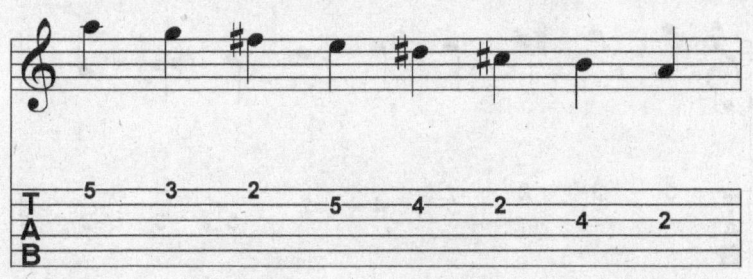

Scale pattern	A B C# D# E F# G A
	A G F# E D# C# B A

A
Diminished

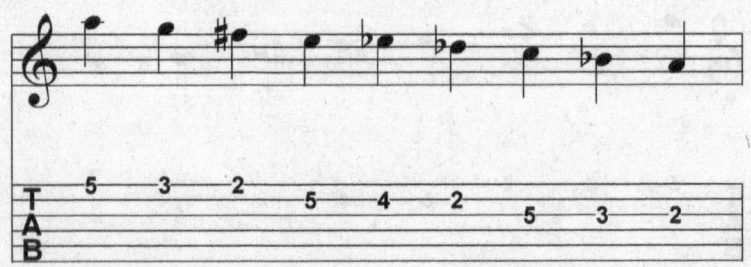

Scale pattern	A B♭ C D♭ E♭ E♮ F♯ G A
	A G F♯ E E♭ D♭ C B♭ A

A
Chromatic

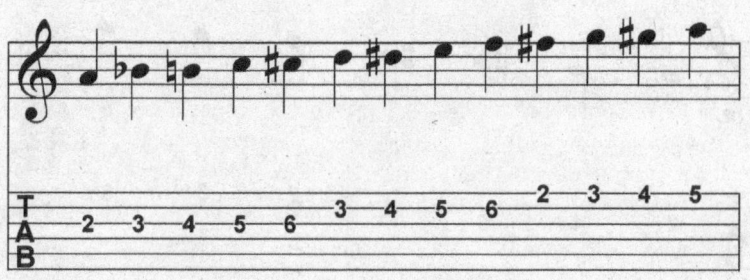

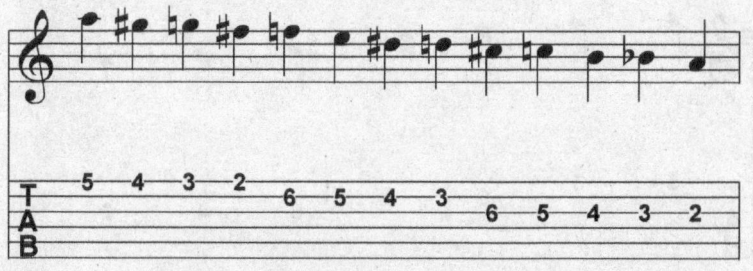

Scale pattern	A B♭ B♮ C C♯ D D♯ E F F♯ G G♯ A
	A G♯ G♮ F♯ F♮ E D♯ D♮ C♯ C♮ B B♭ A

A
Wholetone

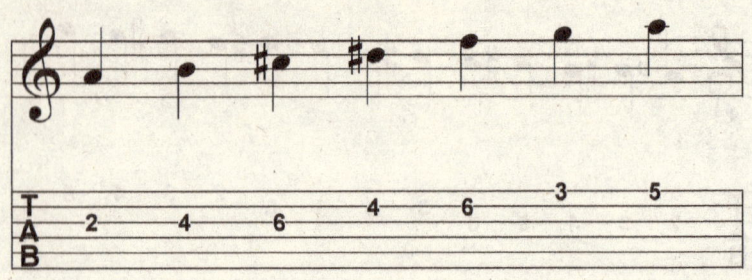

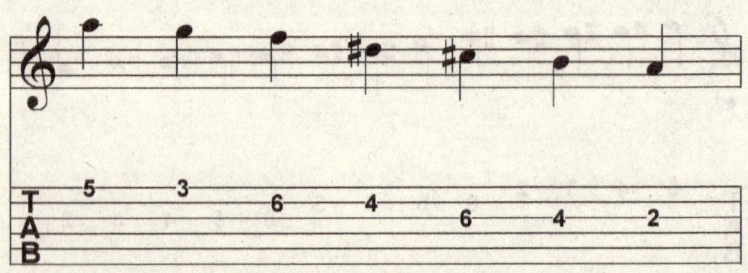

Scale pattern	A B C♯ D♯ F G A
	A G F D♯ C♯ B A

A
Neapolitan

Scale pattern	A Bb C D E F# G# A
	A G# F# E D C Bb A

Online access
flametreemusic.com

Scan the code
to hear the chord

35

A♯/B♭
Major (Ionian Mode)

Scale pattern	B♭ C D E♭ F G A B♭
	B♭ A G F E♭ D C B♭

A♯/B♭
Major Pentatonic

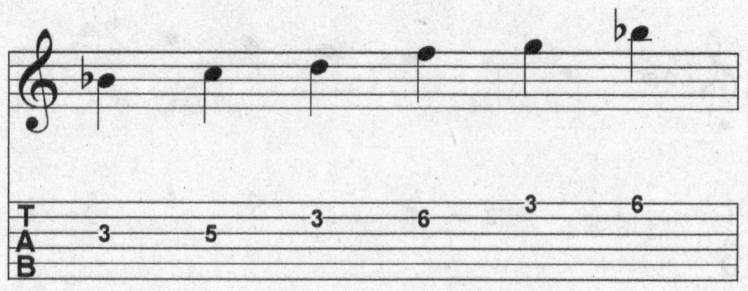

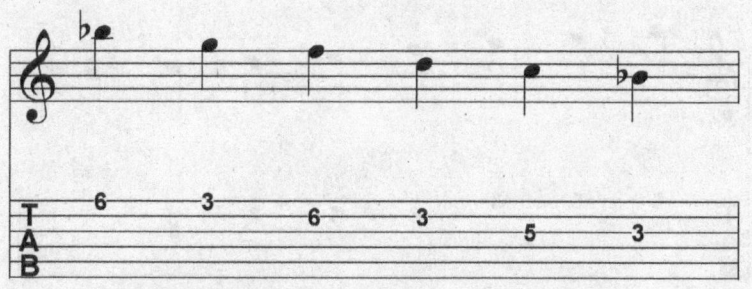

| **Scale pattern** | B♭ C D F G B♭ |
| | B♭ G F D C B♭ |

A♯/B♭
Lydian Mode

Scale pattern	B♭ C D E F G A B♭
	B♭ A G F E D C B♭

A♯/B♭
Lydian Augmented

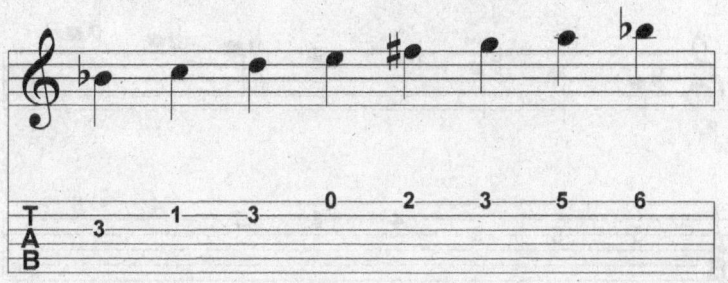

Scale pattern	B♭ C D E F♯ G A B♭
	B♭ A G F♯ E D C B♭

A♯/B♭
Natural Minor (Aeolian)

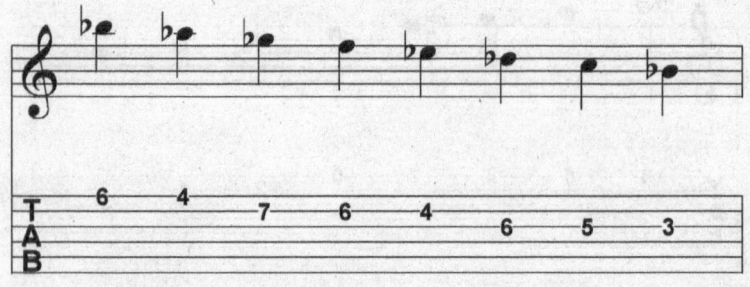

Scale pattern	B♭ C D♭ E♭ F G♭ A♭ B♭
	B♭ A♭ G♭ F E♭ D♭ C B♭

A♯/B♭
Harmonic Minor

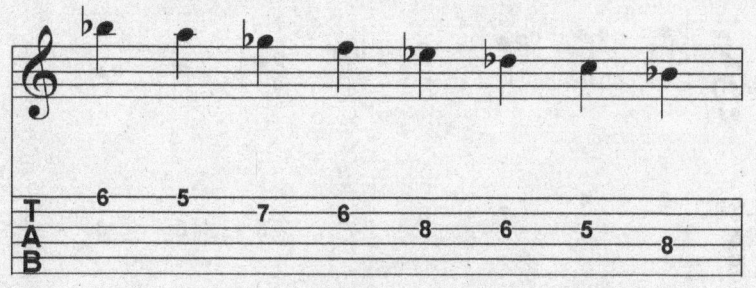

Scale pattern

B♭ C D♭ E♭ F G♭ A B♭
B♭ A G♭ F E♭ D♭ C B♭

A♯/B♭
Melodic Minor

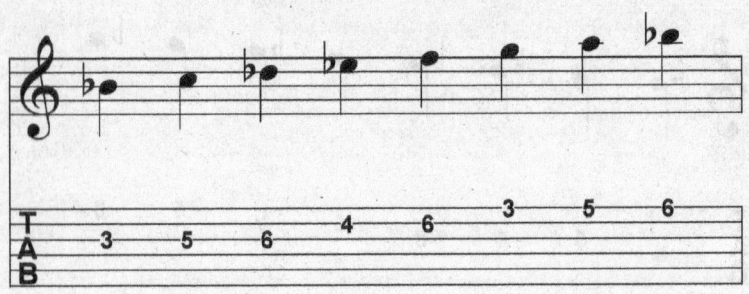

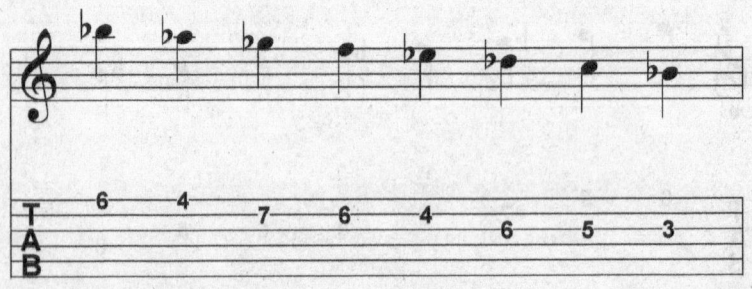

| Scale pattern | B♭ C D♭ E♭ F G A B♭ |
| | B♭ A♭ G♭ F E♭ D♭ C B♭ |

A♯/B♭
Dorian Mode

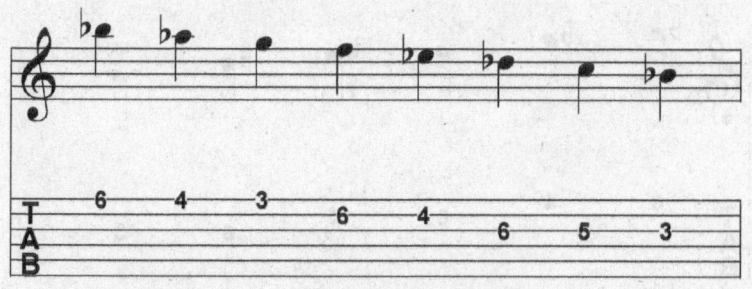

Scale pattern

B♭ C D♭ E♭ F G A♭ B♭
B♭ A♭ G F E♭ D♭ C B♭

A#/B♭
Minor Pentatonic

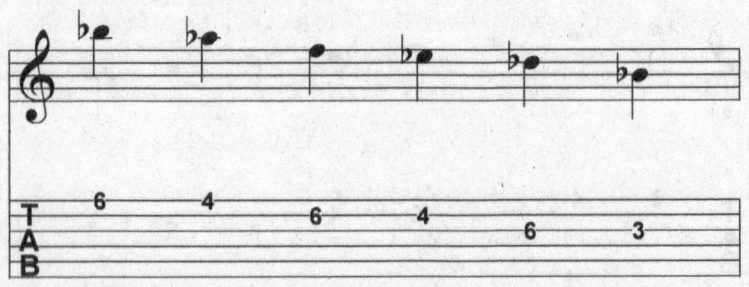

Scale pattern	B♭ D♭ E♭ F A♭ B♭
	B♭ A♭ F E♭ D♭ B♭

Online access
flametreemusic.com

Scan the code
to hear the chord

A♯/B♭
Blues

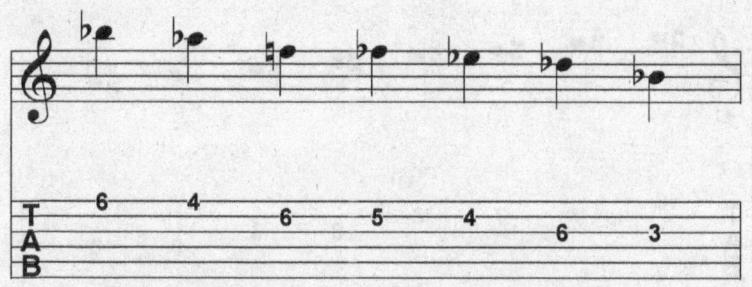

Scale pattern	B♭ D♭ E♭ F♭ F♮ A♭ B♭
	B♭ A♭ F♮ F♭ E♭ D♭ B♭

A♯/B♭
Phrygian Mode

Scale pattern	A♯ B C♯ D♯ E♯ F♯ G♯ A♯
	A♯ G♯ F♯ E♯ D♯ C♯ B A♯

A♯/B♭
Locrian Mode

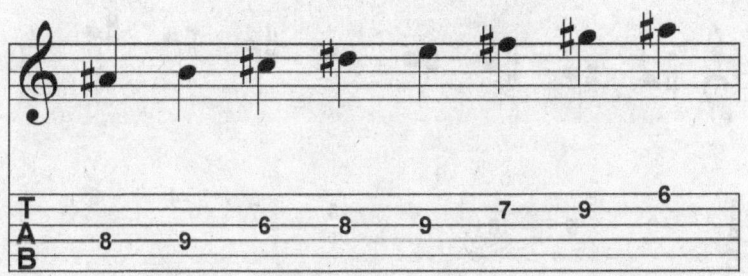

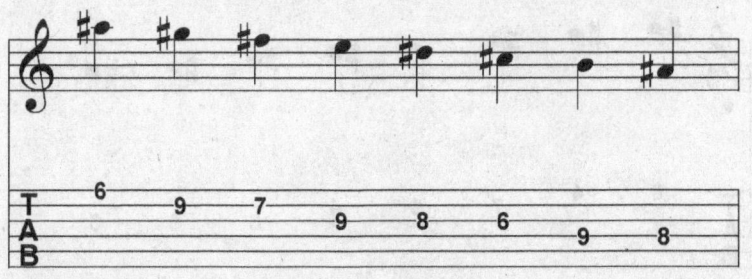

| Scale pattern | A♯ B C♯ D♯ E F♯ G♯ A♯ |
| | A♯ G♯ F♯ E D♯ C♯ B A♯ |

A♯/B♭
Half-diminished

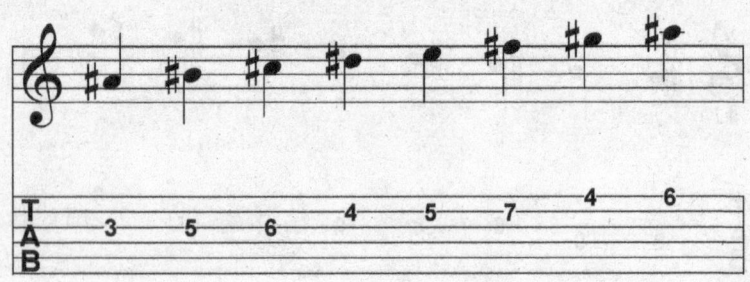

Scale pattern	A♯ B♯ C♯ D♯ E F♯ G♯ A♯
	A♯ G♯ F♯ E D♯ C♯ B♯ A♯

A♯/B♭
Mixolydian Mode

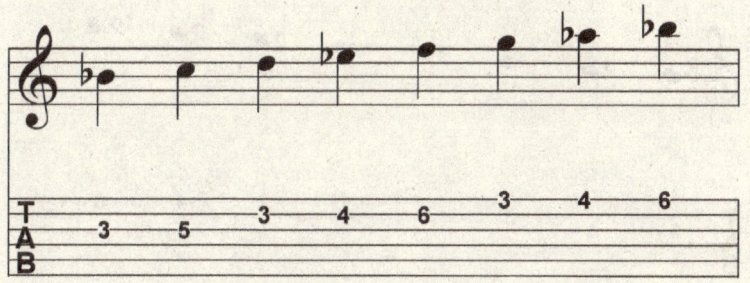

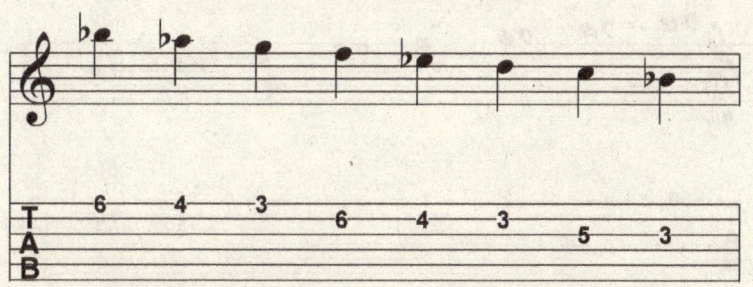

Scale pattern	B♭ C D E♭ F G A♭ B♭
	B♭ A♭ G F E♭ D C B♭

A♯/B♭
Phrygian Major/Spanish

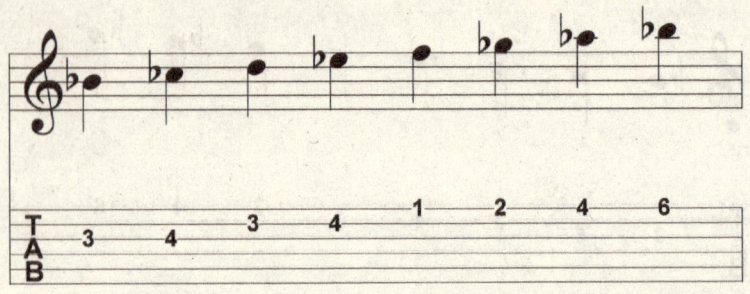

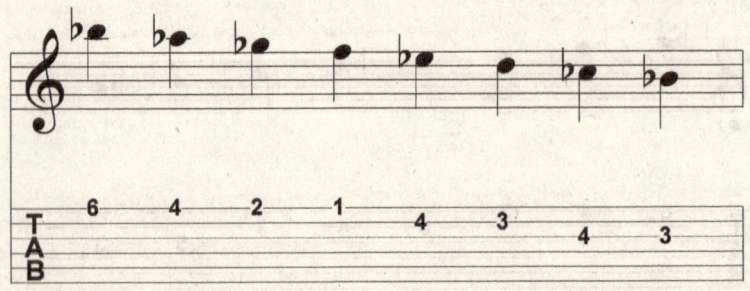

Scale pattern	B♭ C♭ D E♭ F G♭ A♭ B♭
	B♭ A♭ G♭ F E♭ D C♭ B♭

A♯/B♭
Lydian Dominant

Scale pattern	B♭ C D E F G A♭ B♭
	B♭ A♭ G F E D C B♭

A♯/B♭
Diminished

Scale pattern	B♭ C♭ D♭ D♮ E F G A♭ B♭
	B♭ A♭ G F E D♮ D♭ C♭ B♭

A♯/B♭
Chromatic

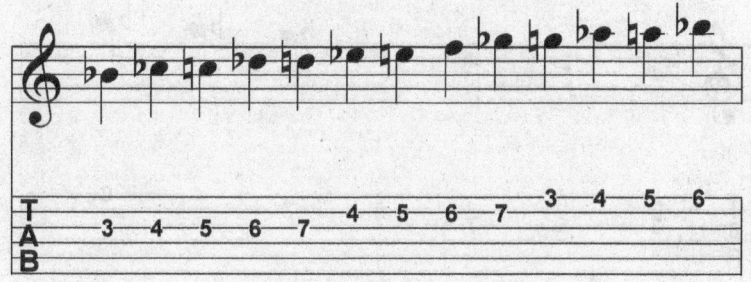

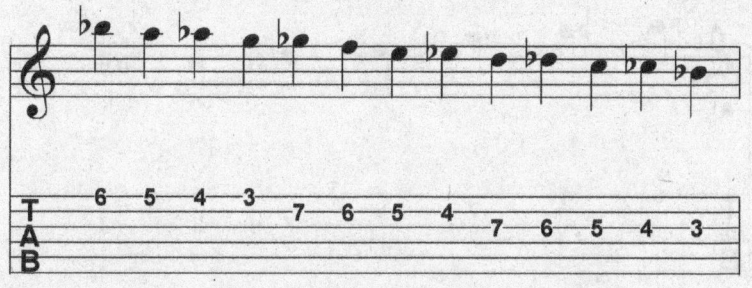

Scale pattern

B♭ C♭ C♮ D♭ D♮ E♭ E♮ F G♭ G♮ A♭ A♮ B♭
B♭ A A♭ G G♭ F E E♭ D D♭ C C♭ B♭

A#/B♭
Wholetone

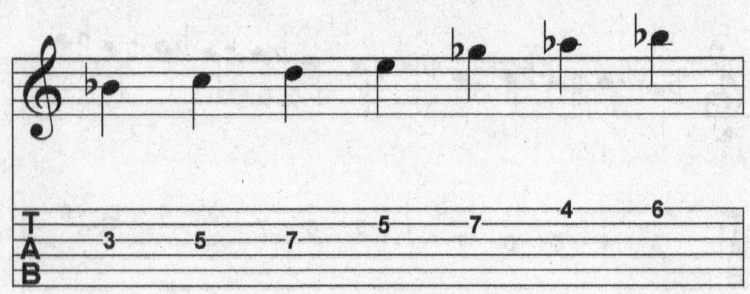

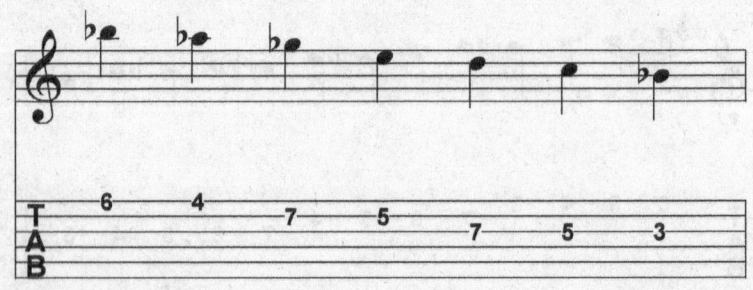

Scale pattern	B♭ C D E G♭ A♭ B♭
	B♭ A♭ G♭ E D C B♭

A♯/B♭
Neapolitan

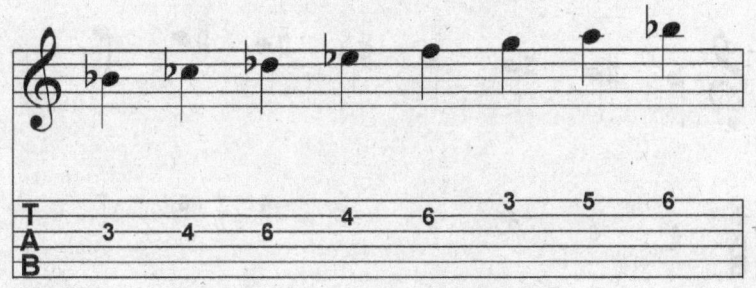

| Scale pattern | B♭ C♭ D♭ E♭ F G A B♭ |
| | B♭ A G F E♭ D♭ C♭ B♭ |

B

Major (Ionian Mode)

Scale pattern	B C# D# E F# G# A# B
	B A# G# F# E D# C# B

B
Major Pentatonic

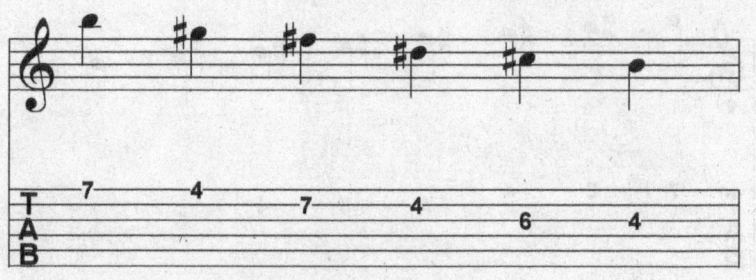

Scale pattern

B C# D# F# G# B
B G# F# D# C# B

B
Lydian Mode

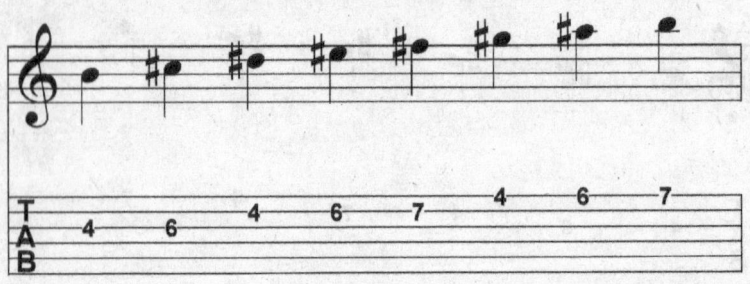

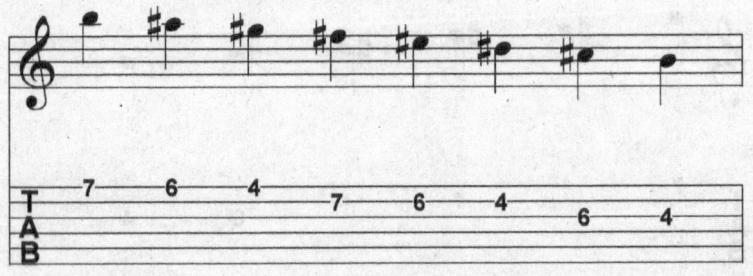

Scale pattern	B C# D# E# F# G# A# B
	B A# G# F# E# D# C# B

B
Lydian Augmented

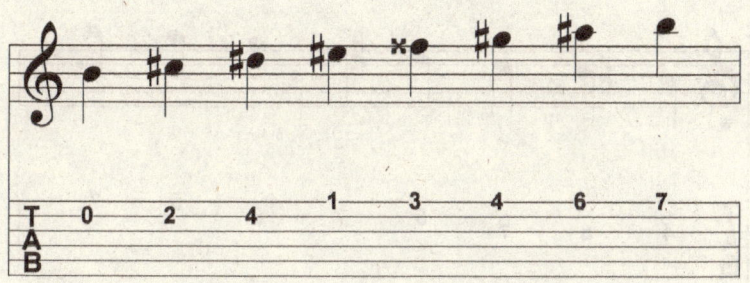

Scale pattern	B C# D# E# F× G# A# B
	B A# G# F× E# D# C# B

B
Natural Minor (Aeolian Mode)

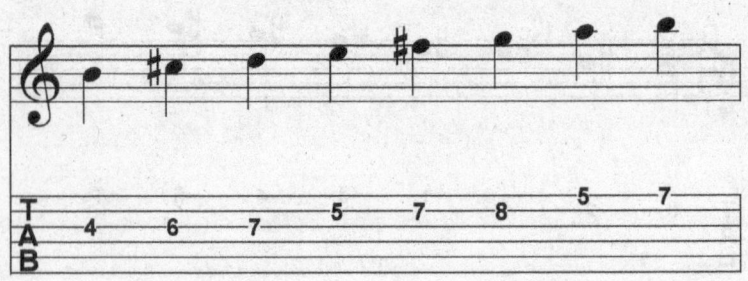

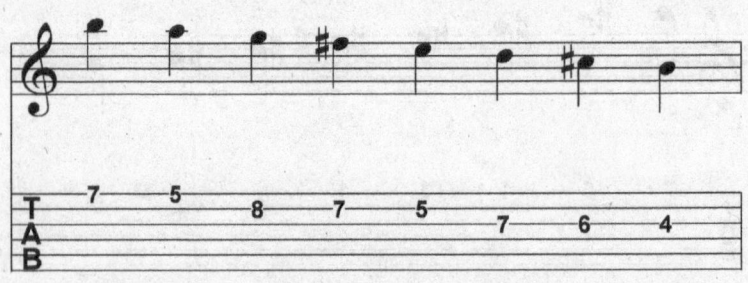

Scale pattern	B C# D E F# G A B
	B A G F# E D C# B

B
Harmonic Minor

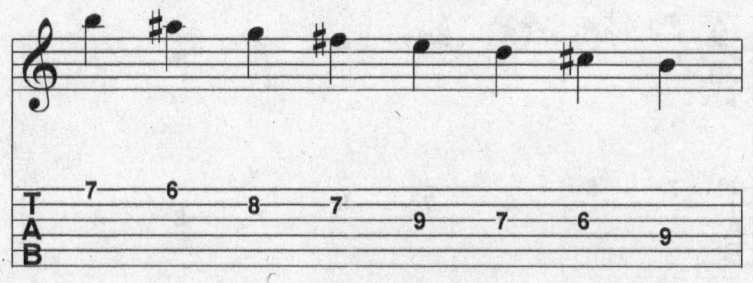

Scale pattern

B C♯ D E F♯ G A♯ B
B A♯ G F♯ E D C♯ B

B
Melodic Minor

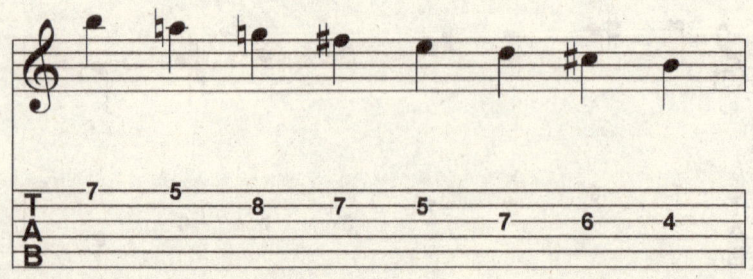

Scale pattern

B C# D E F# G# A# B
B A♮ G♮ F# E D C# B

Online access
flametreemusic.com

Scan the code
to hear the chord

B
Dorian Mode

Scale pattern	B C# D E F# G A B
	B A G# F# E D C# B

Online access
flametreemusic.com

Scan the code
to hear the chord

B

Minor Pentatonic

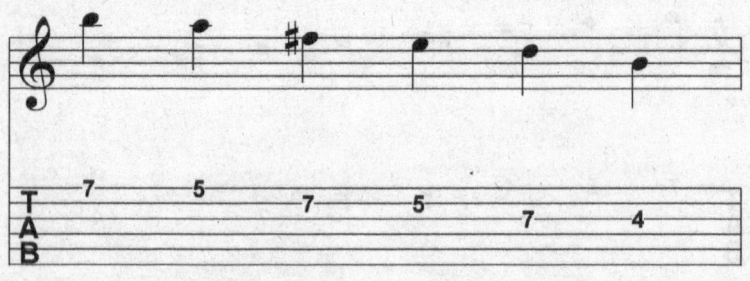

Scale pattern

B D E F♯ A B
B A F♯ E D B

B
Blues

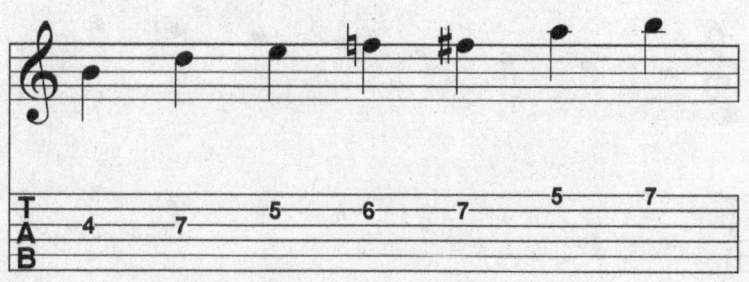

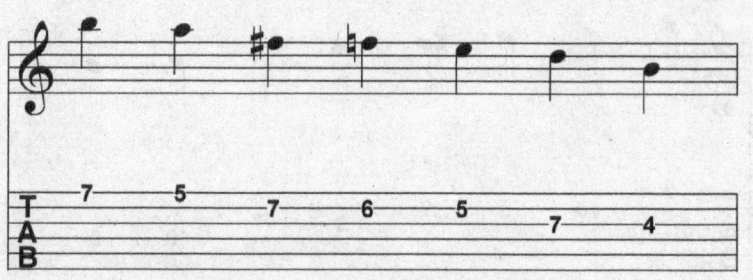

Scale pattern	B D E F♮ F♯ A B
	B A F♯ F♮ E D B

B
Phrygian Mode

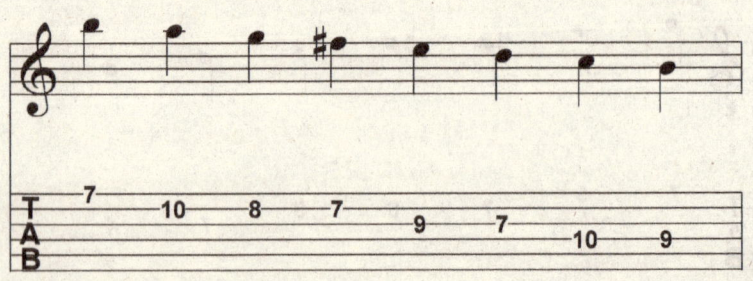

Scale pattern	B C D E F♯ G A B
	B A G F♯ E D C B

Online access
flametreemusic.com

Scan the code
to hear the chord

B
Locrian Mode

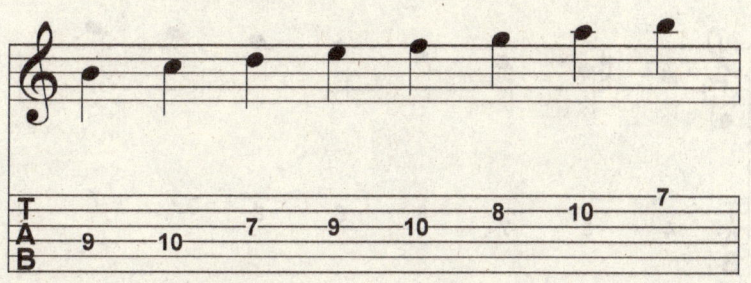

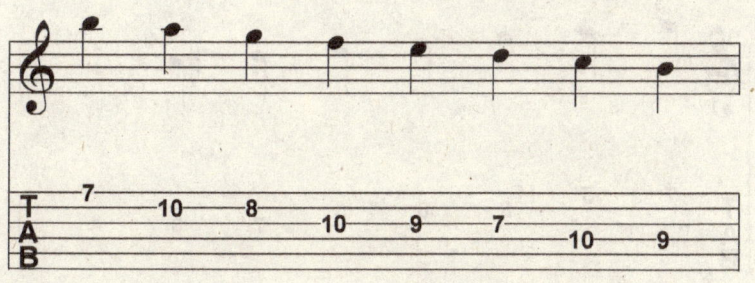

Scale pattern	B C D E F G A B
	B A G F E D C B

Online access
flametreemusic.com Scan the code
to hear the chord

B
Half-diminished

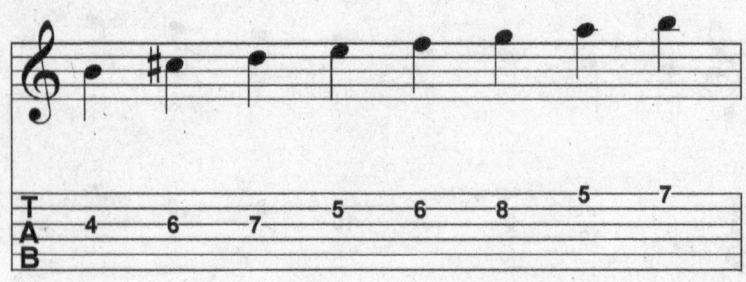

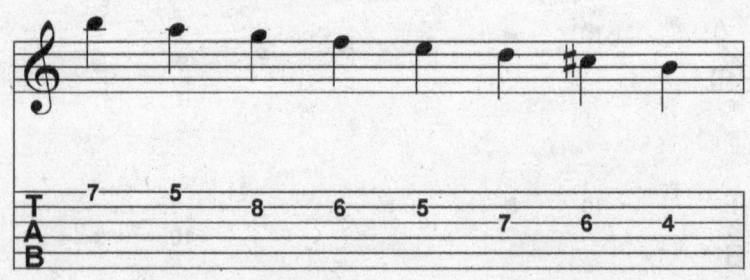

Scale pattern	B C♯ D E F G A B B A G F E D C♯ B

B
Mixolydian Mode

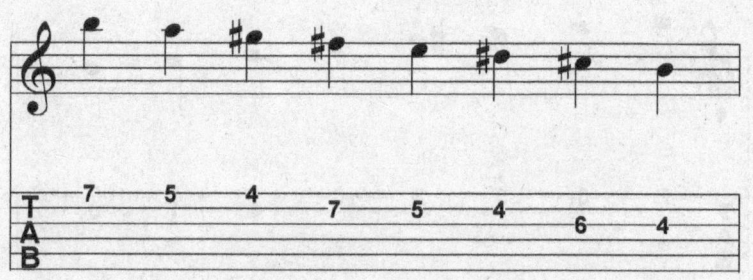

Scale pattern	B C# D# E F# G# A B
	B A G# F# E D# C# B

B
Phrygian Major/Spanish

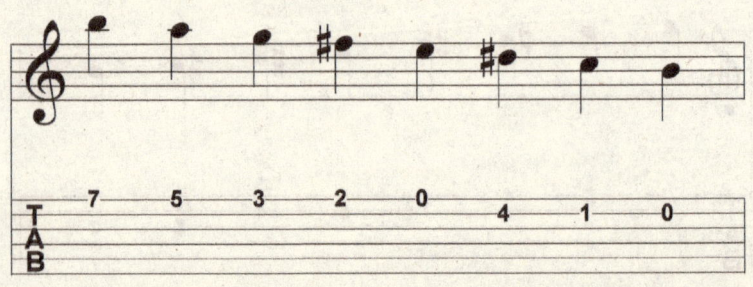

Scale pattern	B C D♯ E F♯ G A B
	B A G F♯ E D♯ C B

B
Lydian Dominant

Scale pattern	B C# D# E# F# G# A B
	B A G# F# E# D# C# B

Online access
flametreemusic.com

Scan the code
to hear the chord

B
Diminished

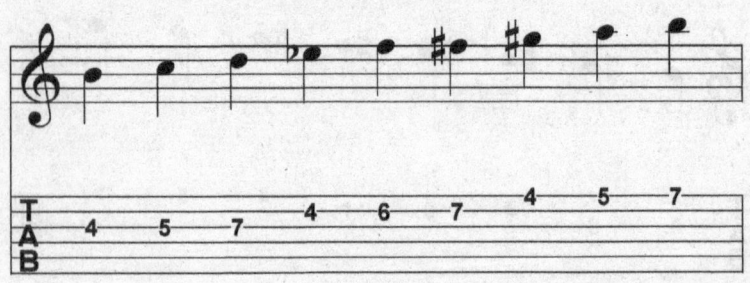

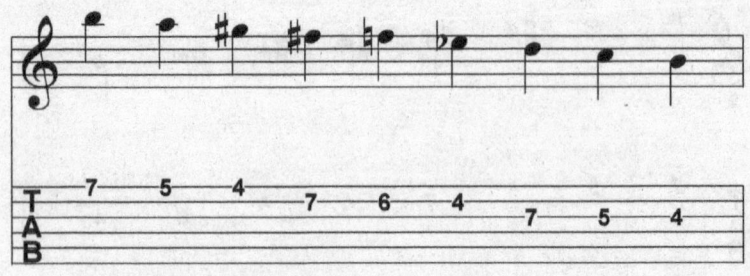

Scale pattern	B C D E♭ F F♯ G♯ A B
	B A G♯ F♯ F♮ E♭ D C B

B
Chromatic

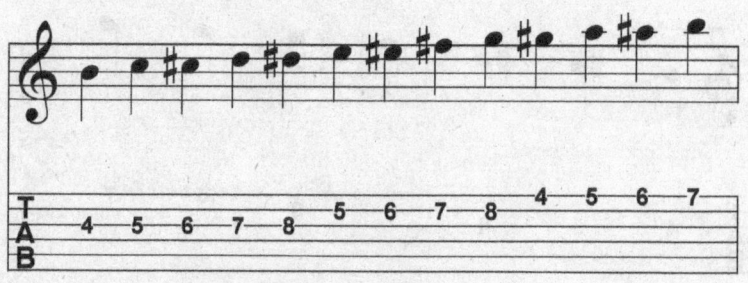

| Scale pattern | B C C# D D# E E# F# G G# A A# B |
| | B A# A♭ G# G♮ F# E# E♮ D# D♮ C# C♮ B |

B
Wholetone

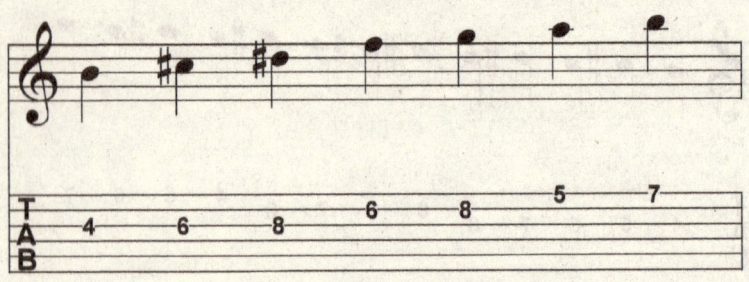

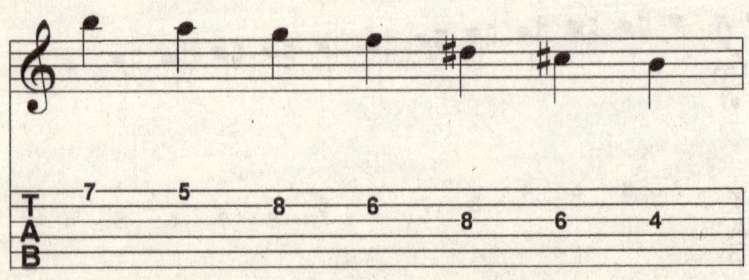

Scale pattern	B C# D# F G A B
	B A G F D# C# B

B
Neapolitan

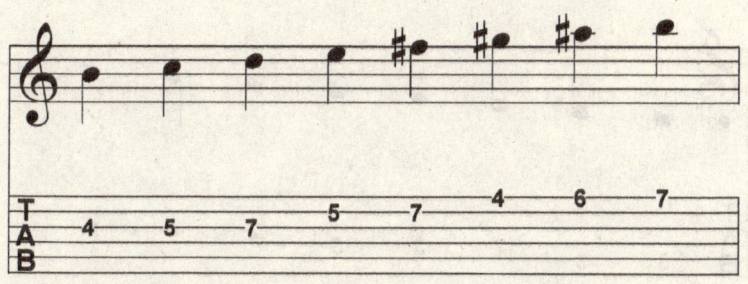

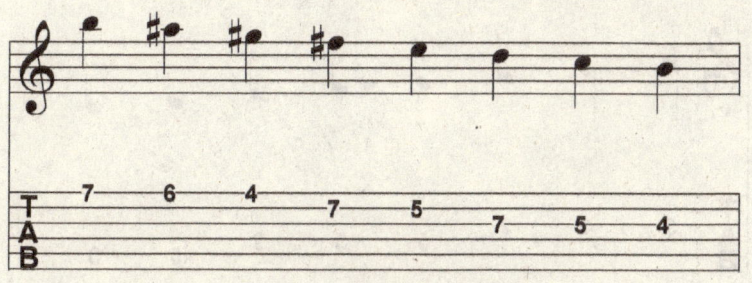

| Scale pattern | B C D E F# G# A# B |
| | B A# G# F# E D C B |

C
Major (Ionian mode)

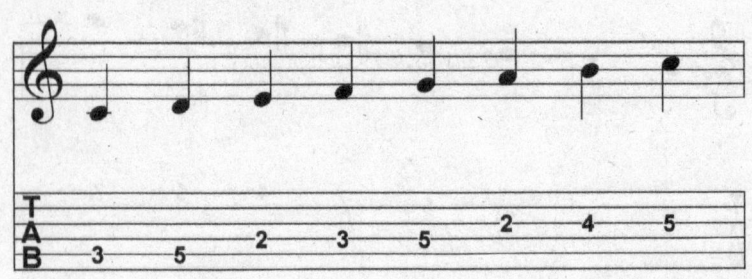

Scale pattern	C D E F G A B C
	C B A G F E D C

C
Major Pentatonic

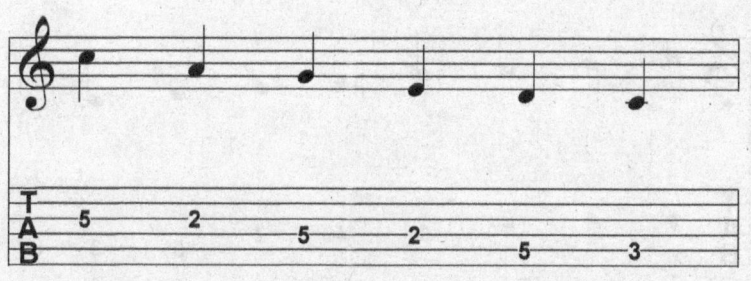

Scale pattern	C D E G A C
	C A G E D C

C
Lydian Mode

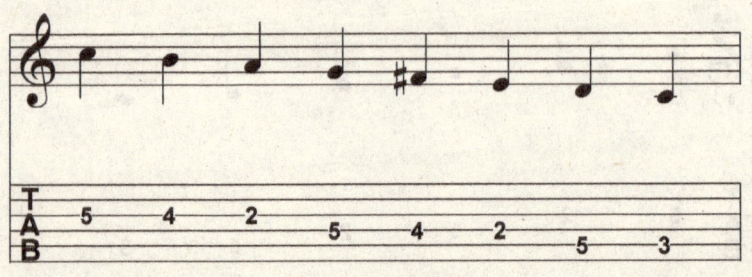

| **Scale pattern** | C D E F♯ G A B C
C B A G F♯ E D C |

C
Lydian Augmented

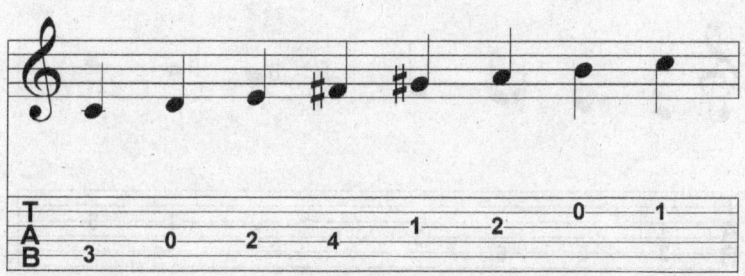

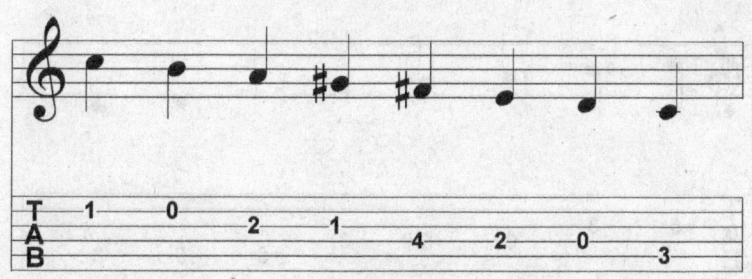

Scale pattern	C D E F♯ G♯ A B C
	C B A G♯ F♯ E D C

C

Natural Minor (Aeolian mode)

Scale pattern	C D E♭ F G A♭ B♭ C
	C B♭ A♭ G F E♭ D C

C
Harmonic Minor

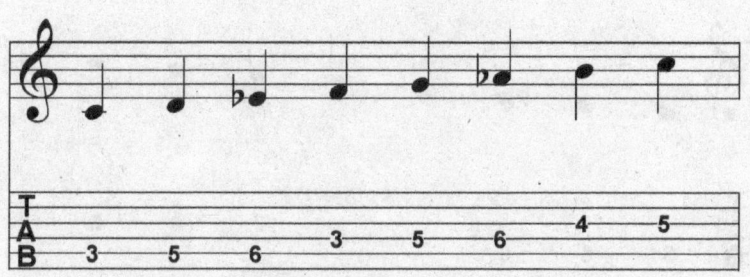

Scale pattern	C D E♭ F G A♭ B C
	C B A♭ G F E♭ D C

C
Melodic Minor

Scale pattern	C D E♭ F G A B C
	C B♭ A♭ G F E♭ D C

C
Dorian Mode

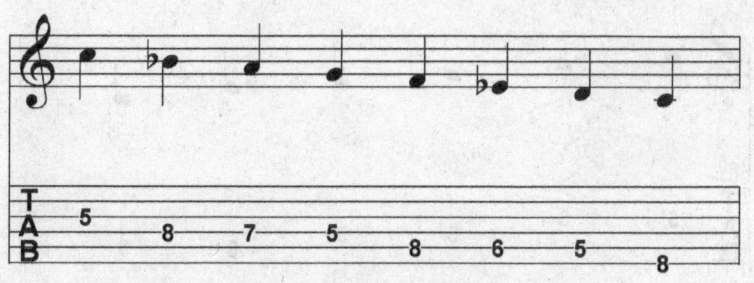

Scale pattern	C D E♭ F G A B♭ C
	C B♭ A G F E♭ D C

C
Minor Pentatonic

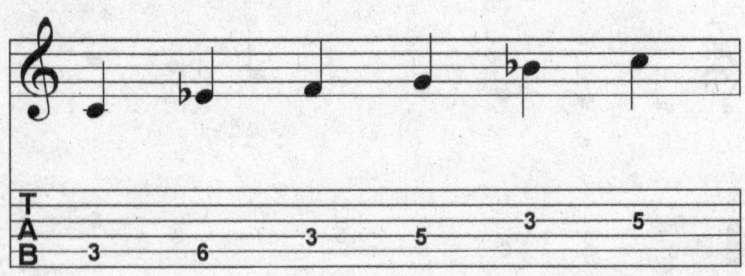

| **Scale pattern** | C B♭ F G B♭ C |
| | C B♭ G F E♭ C |

C
Blues

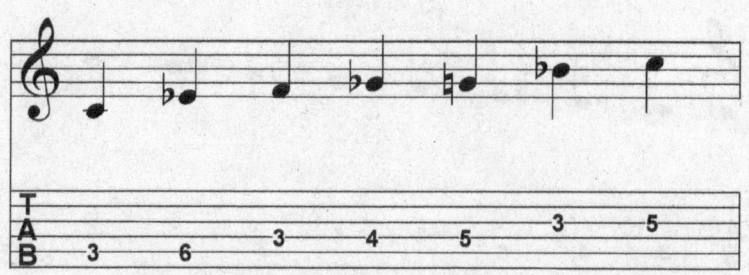

| Scale pattern | C E♭ F G♭ G♮ B♭ C |
| | C B♭ G♮ G♭ F E♭ C |

Online access
flametreemusic.com

Scan the code
to hear the chord

C
Phrygian Mode

Scale pattern	C Db Eb F G Ab Bb C
	C Bb Ab G F Eb Db C

C
Locrian Mode

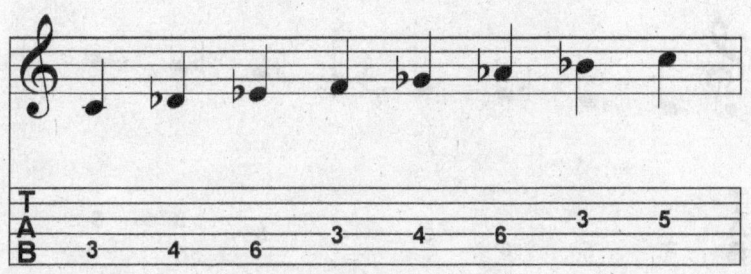

Scale pattern	C Db Eb F Gb Ab Bb C
	C Bb Ab Gb F Eb Db C

Online access
flametreemusic.com

Scan the code
to hear the chord

C
Half-diminished

Scale pattern	C D E♭ F G♭ A♭ B♭ C
	C B♭ A♭ G♭ F E♭ D C

Online access
flametreemusic.com Scan the code
to hear the chord

C
Mixolydian Mode

Scale pattern	C D E F G A B♭ C
	C B♭ A G F E D C

C
Phrygian Major/Spanish

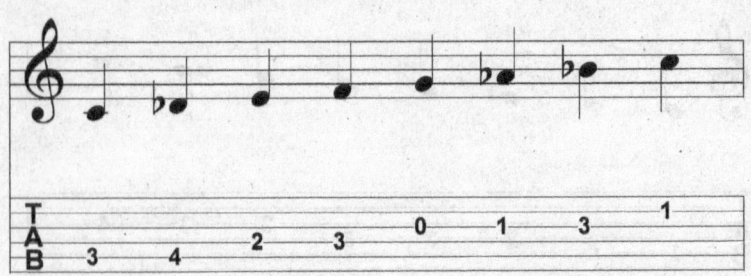

| **Scale pattern** | C D♭ E F G A♭ B♭ C |
| | C B♭ A♭ G F E D♭ C |

C
Lydian Dominant

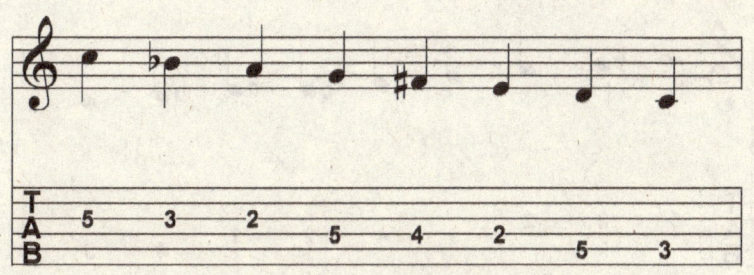

Scale pattern	C D E F♯ G A B♭ C
	C B♭ A G F♯ E D C

C
Diminished

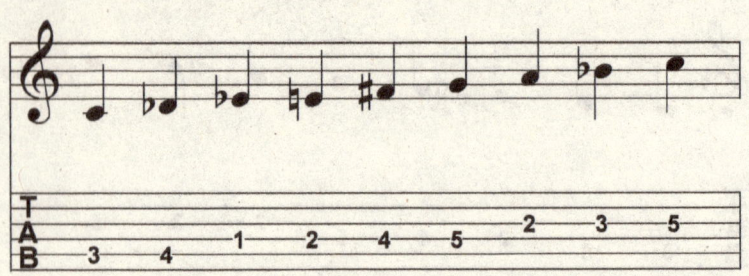

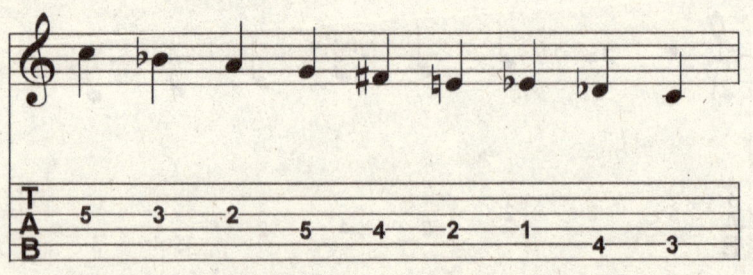

Scale pattern	C D♭ E♭ E♮ F♯ G A B C
	C B♭ A G F♯ E♮ E♭ D♭ C

C
Chromatic

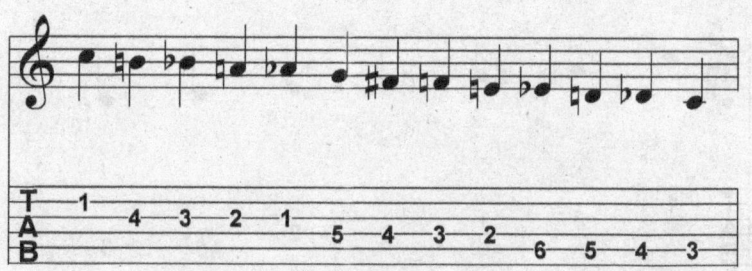

Scale pattern	C D♭ D♮ E♭ E♮ F F♯ G A♭ A♮ B♭ B♮ C
	C B♮ B♭ A♮ A♭ G F♯ F♮ E♭ E♭ D♮ D♭ C

C
Wholetone

Scale pattern	C D E F# G# A# C
	C A# G# F# E D C

C
Neapolitan

Scale pattern	C D♭ E♭ F G A B C
	C B A G F E♭ D♭ C

C#/D♭
Major (Ionian Mode)

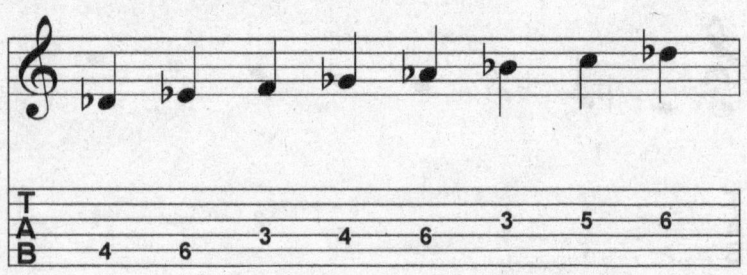

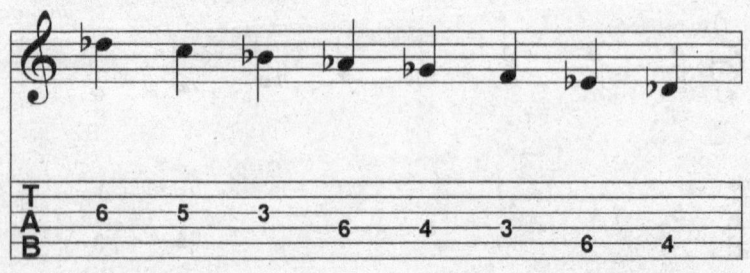

Scale pattern	D♭ E♭ F G♭ A♭ B♭ C D♭
	D♭ C B♭ A♭ G♭ F E♭ D♭

C#/Db
Major Pentatonic

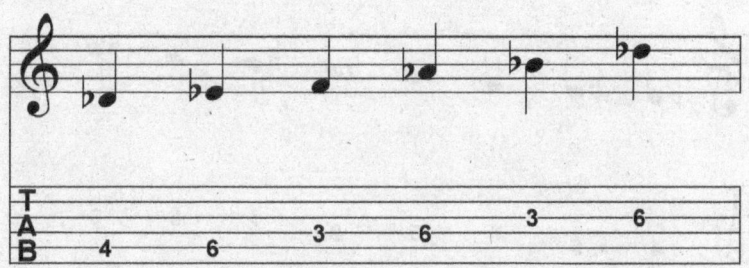

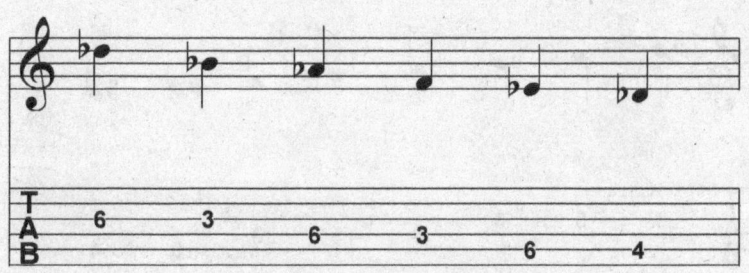

| **Scale pattern** | Db Eb F Ab Bb Db |
| | Db Bb Ab F Eb Db |

C#/D♭
Lydian Mode

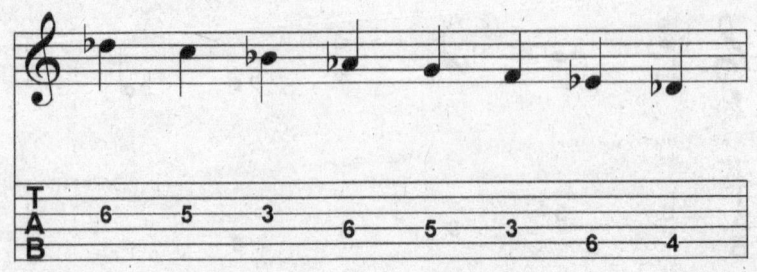

Scale pattern	D♭ E♭ F G A♭ B♭ C D♭
	D♭ C B♭ A♭ G F E♭ D♭

C♯/D♭
Lydian Augmented

Scale pattern	D♭ E♭ F G A B♭ C D♭
	D♭ C B♭ A G F E♭ D♭

C#/D♭
Natural Minor (Aeolian Mode)

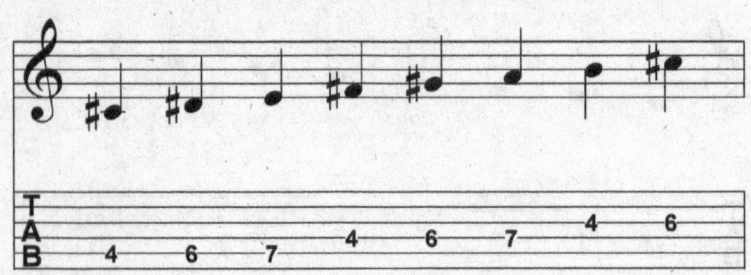

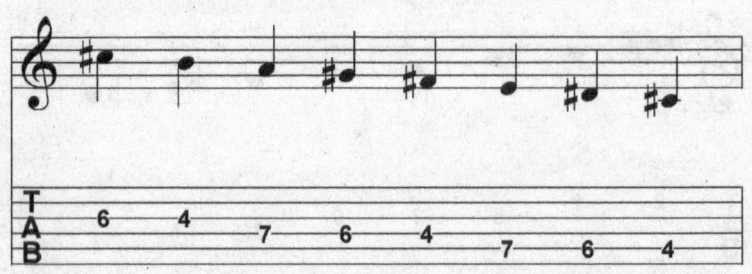

Scale pattern	C# D# E F# G# A B C#
	C# B A G# F# E D# C#

C#/D♭
Harmonic Minor

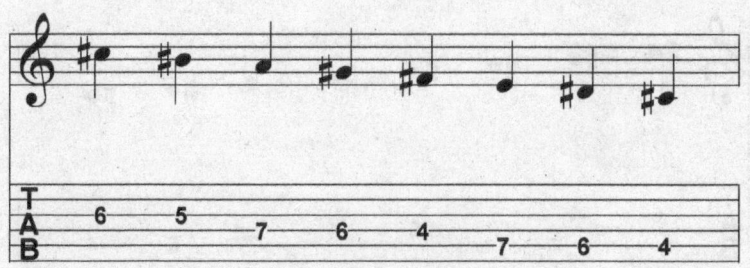

Scale pattern	C# D# E F# G# A B# C#
	C# B# A G# F# E D# C#

C♯/D♭
Melodic Minor

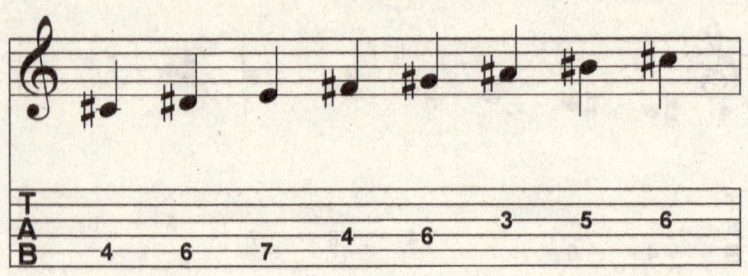

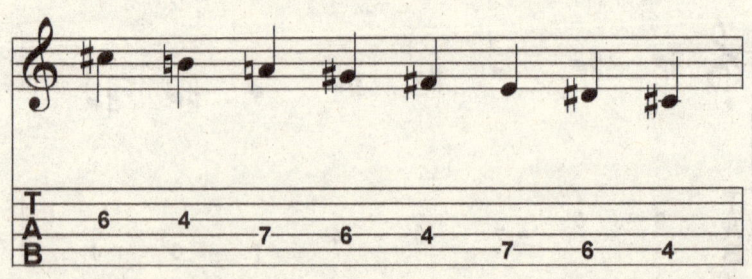

| **Scale pattern** | C♯ D♯ E F♯ G♯ A♯ B♯ C♯ |
| | C♯ B♮ A♮ G♯ F♯ E D♯ C♯ |

C#/D♭
Dorian Mode

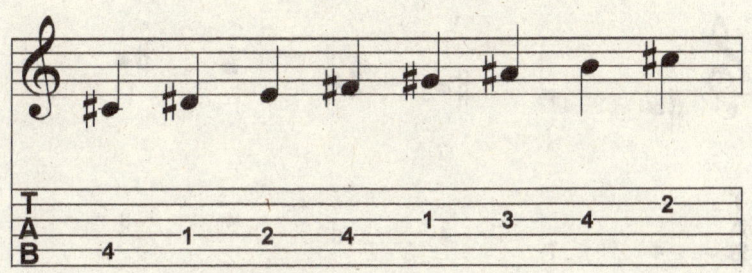

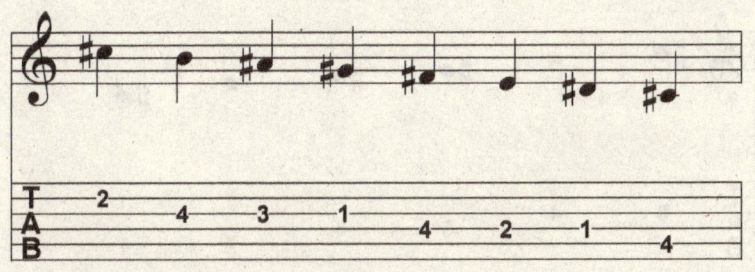

Scale pattern	C# D# E F# G# A# B C# C# B A# G# F# E D# C#

C♯/D♭
Minor Pentatonic

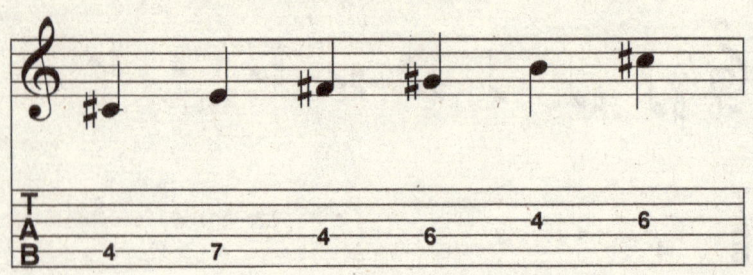

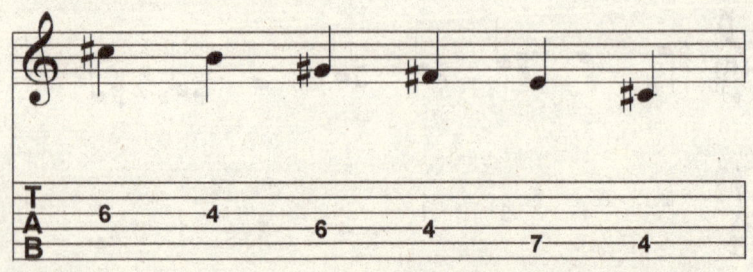

Scale pattern	C♯ E F♯ G♯ B C♯
	C♯ B G♯ F♯ E C♯

C#/D♭
Blues

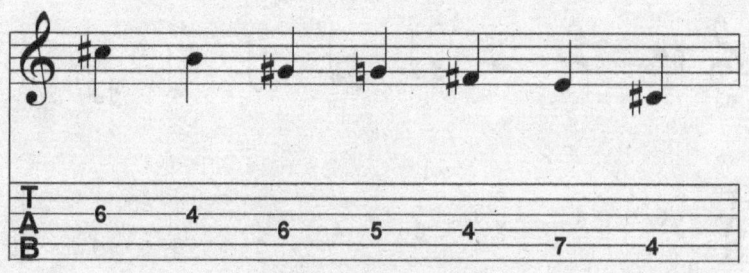

Scale pattern	C# E F# G♮ G# B C#
	C# B G# G♮ F# E C#

C#/Db
Phrygian Mode

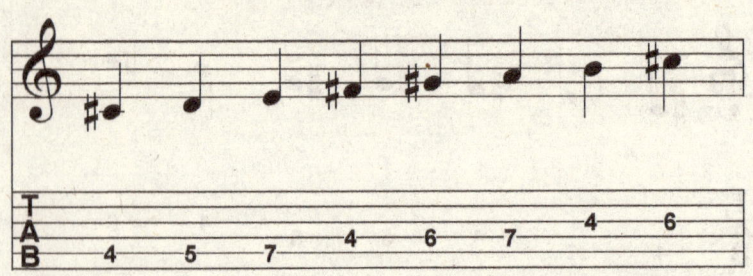

Scale pattern	C# D E F# G# A B C#
	C# B A G# F# E D C#

C#/D♭
Locrian Mode

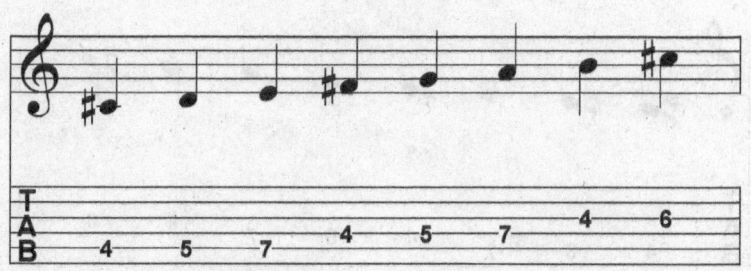

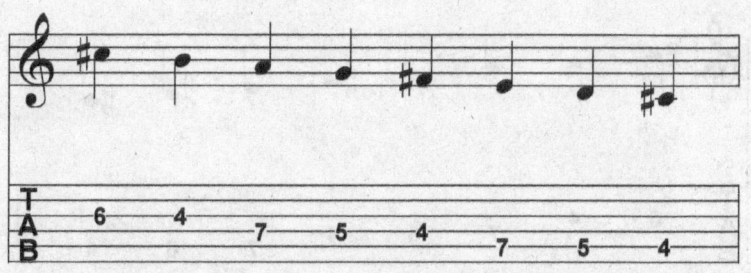

Scale pattern	C# D E F# G A B C# C# B A G F# E D C#

C#/D♭
Half-diminished

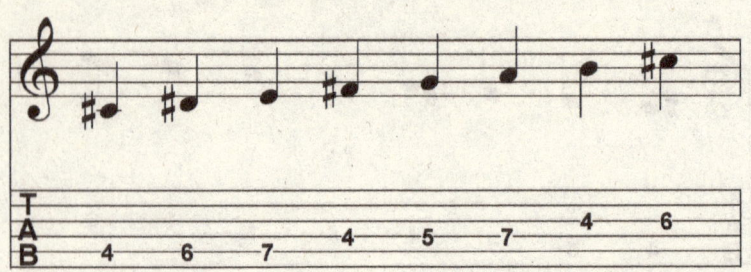

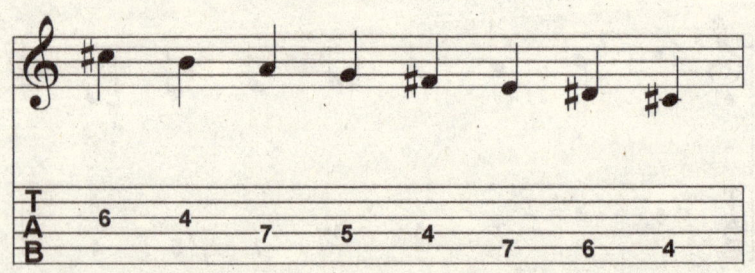

Scale pattern	C# D# E F# G A B C#
	C# B A G F# E D# C#

C♯/D♭
Mixolydian Mode

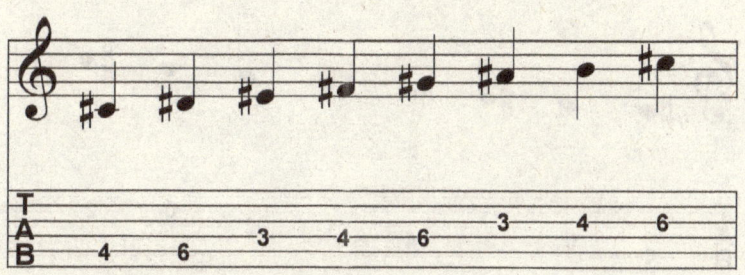

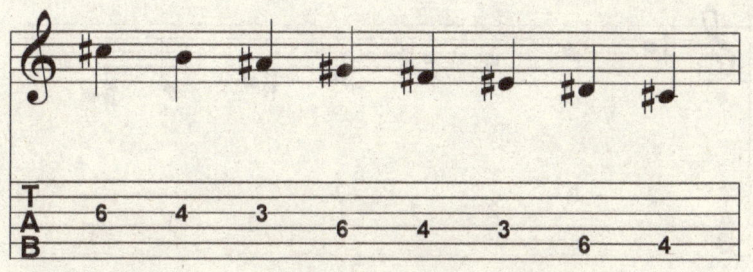

Scale pattern	C♯ D♯ E♯ F♯ G♯ A♯ B C♯
	C♯ B A♯ G♯ F♯ E♯ D♯ C♯

C♯/D♭
Phrygian Major/Spanish

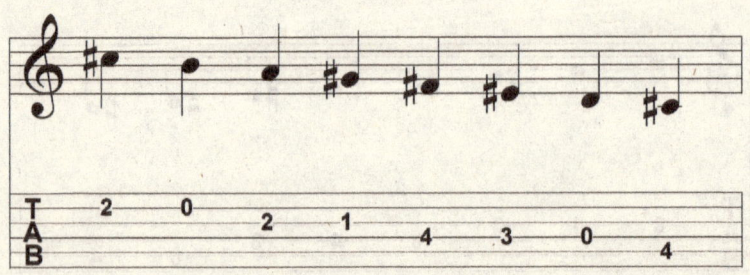

| **Scale pattern** | C♯ D E♯ F♯ G♯ A B C♯ |
| | C♯ B A G♯ F♯ E♯ D C♯ |

C#/D♭
Lydian Dominant

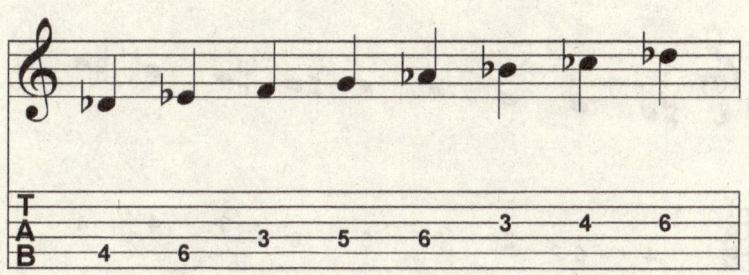

Scale pattern	D♭ E♭ F G A♭ B♭ C♭ D♭
	D♭ C♭ B♭ A♭ G F E♭ D♭

C#/D♭
Diminished

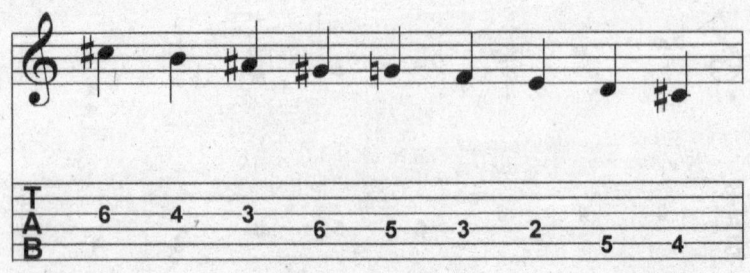

Scale pattern	C# D E F G G# A# B C# C# B A# G# G♮ F E D C#

C♯/D♭
Chromatic

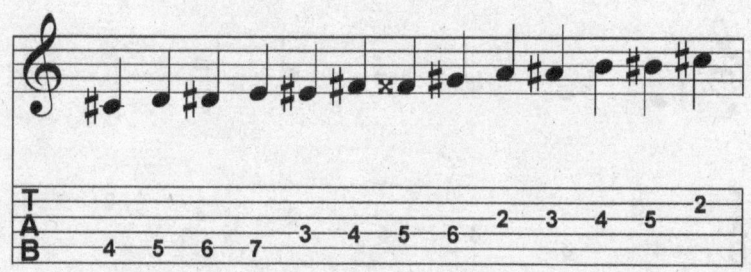

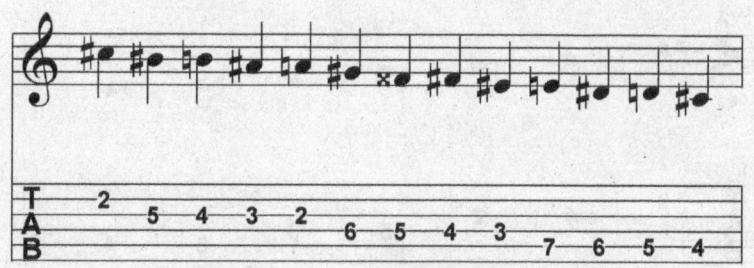

Scale pattern

C♯ D D♯ E E♯ F♯ F× G♯ A A♯ B B♯ C♯
C♯ B♯ B♮ A♯ A♮ G♯ F× F♯ E♯ E♮ D♯ D♮ C♯

C#/D♭
Wholetone

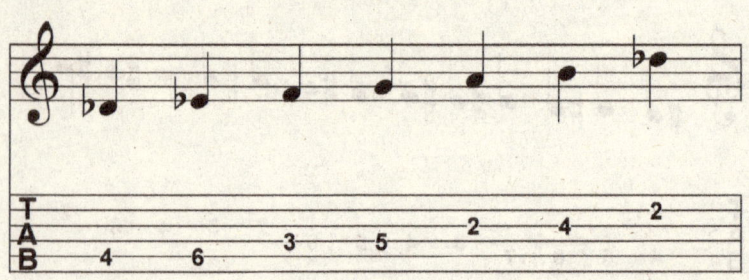

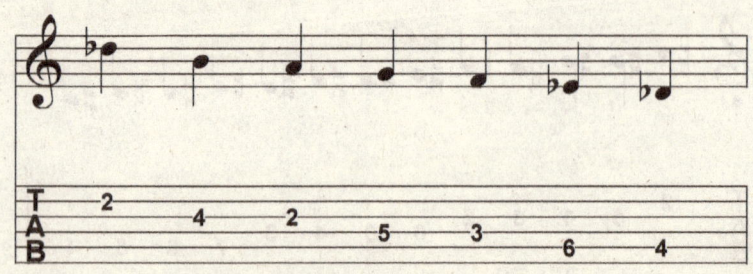

Scale pattern	D♭ E♭ F G A B D♭
	D♭ B A G F E♭ D♭

C♯/D♭
Neapolitan

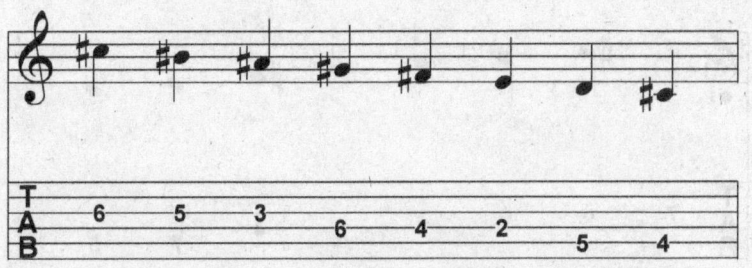

Scale pattern	C♯ D E F♯ G♯ A♯ B♯ C♯
	C♯ B♯ A♯ G♯ F♯ E D C♯

Online access
flametreemusic.com Scan the code
to hear the chord

D
Major (Ionian Mode)

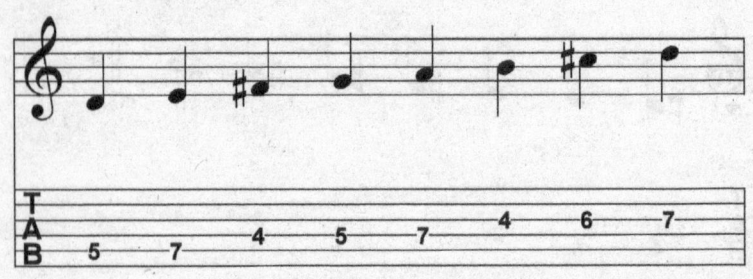

Scale pattern	D E F# G A B C# D D C# B A G F# E D

D
Major Pentatonic

Scale pattern	D E F# A B D
	D B A F# E D

D
Lydian Mode

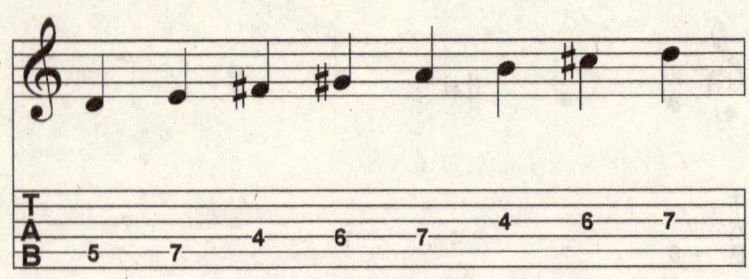

Scale pattern

D E F# G# A B C# D
D C# B A G# F# E D

D
Lydian Augmented

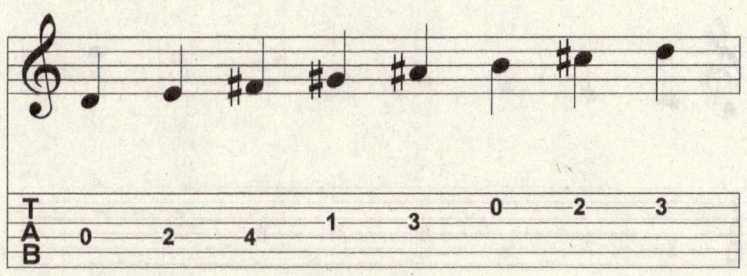

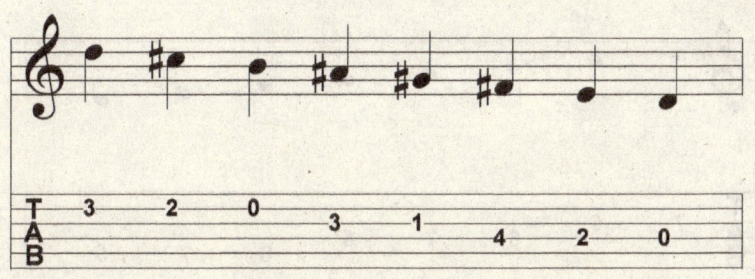

Scale pattern	D E F♯ G♯ A♯ B C♯ D
	D C♯ B A♯ G♯ F♯ E D

D
Natural Minor (Aeolian Mode)

Scale pattern	D E F G A B♭ C D D C B♭ A G F E D

D
Harmonic Minor

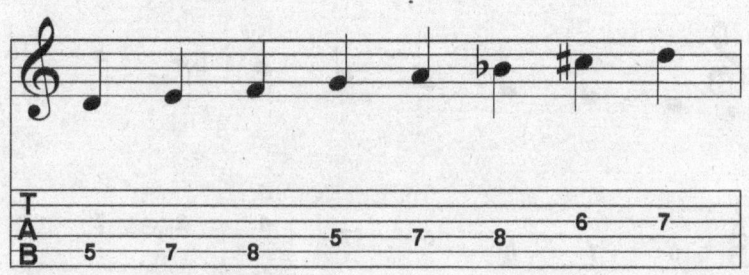

| Scale pattern | D E F G A B♭ C♯ D |
| | D C♯ B♭ A G F E D |

Online access
flametreemusic.com

Scan the code
to hear the chord

D
Melodic Minor

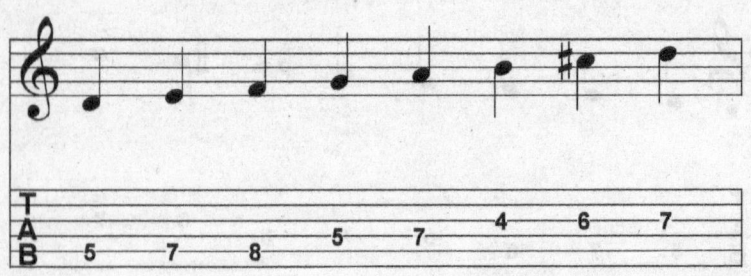

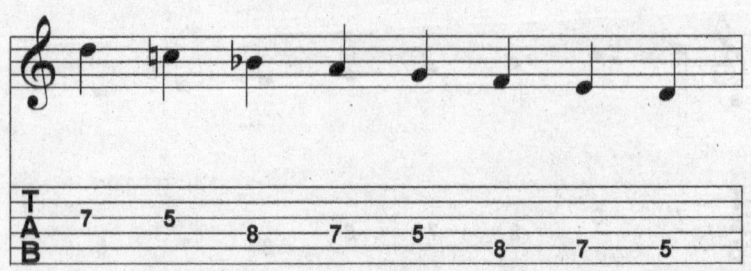

| Scale pattern | D E F G A B C♯ D |
| | D C♮ B♭ A G F E D |

D
Dorian Mode

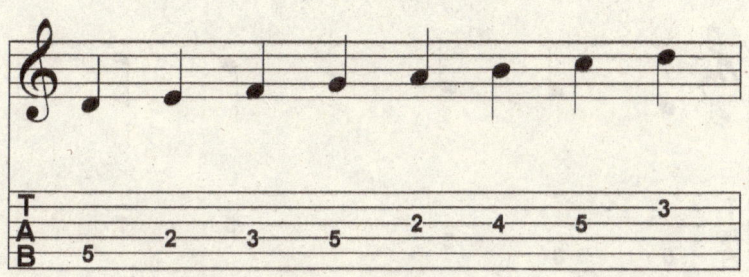

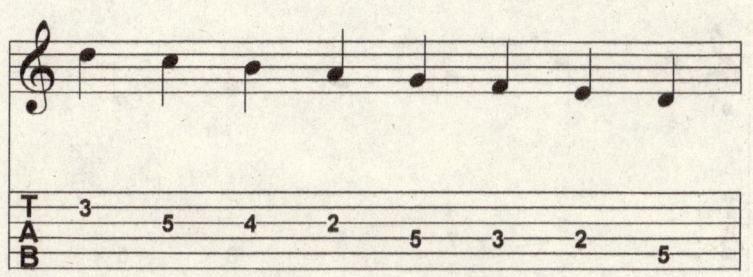

Scale pattern	D E F G A B C D D C B A G F E D

D
Minor Pentatonic

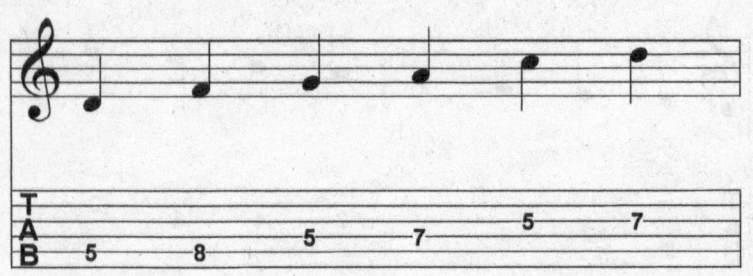

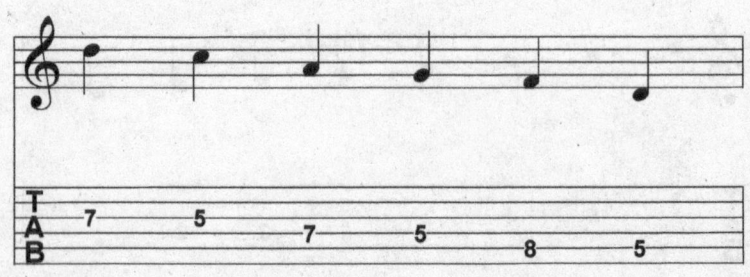

Scale pattern	D F G A C D D C A G F D

D
Blues

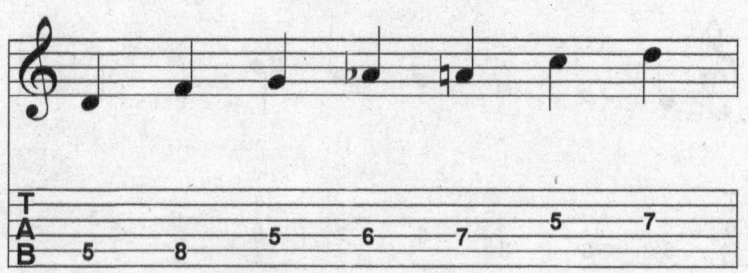

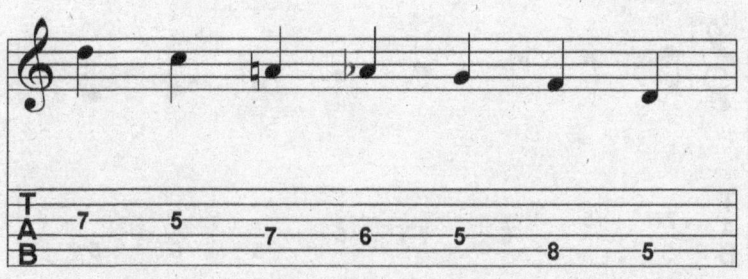

Scale pattern	D F G A♭ A♮ C D
	D C A♮ A♭ G F D

D
Phrygian Mode

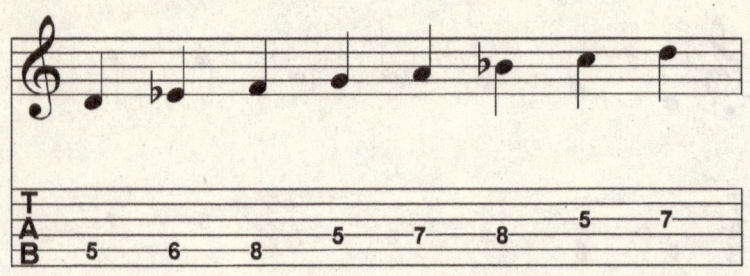

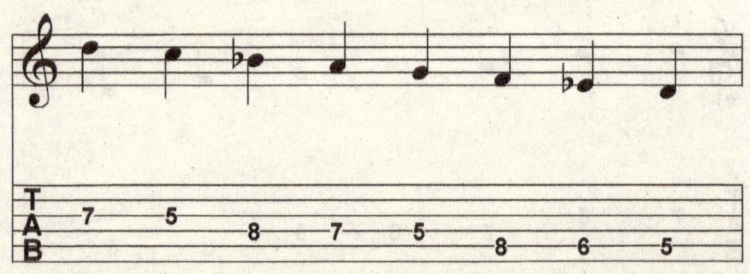

Scale pattern	D E♭ F G A B♭ C D
	D C B♭ A G F E♭ D

Online access
flametreemusic.com

Scan the code
to hear the chord

D
Locrian Mode

Scale pattern	D E♭ F G A♭ B♭ C D D C B♭ A♭ G F E♭ D

D
Half-diminished

Scale pattern	D E F G A♭ B♭ C D
	D C B♭ A♭ G F E D

D
Mixolydian Mode

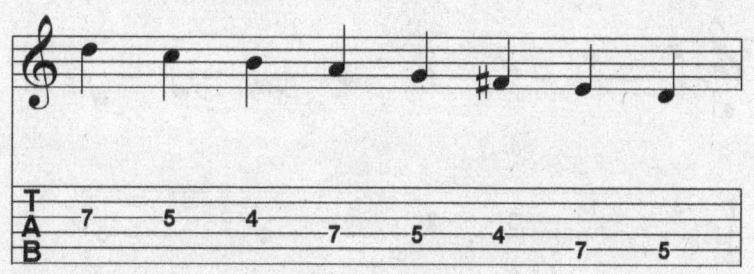

Scale pattern	D E F# G A B C D
	D C B A G F# E D

D
Phrygian Major/Spanish

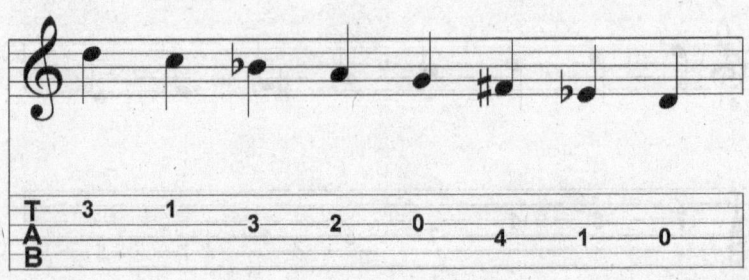

| Scale pattern | D E♭ F♯ G A B♭ C D |
| | D C B♭ A G F♯ E♭ D |

D
Lydian Dominant

| Scale pattern | D E F♯ G♯ A B C D |
| | D C B A G♯ F♯ E D |

Online access
flametreemusic.com   Scan the code
to hear the chord

D
Diminished

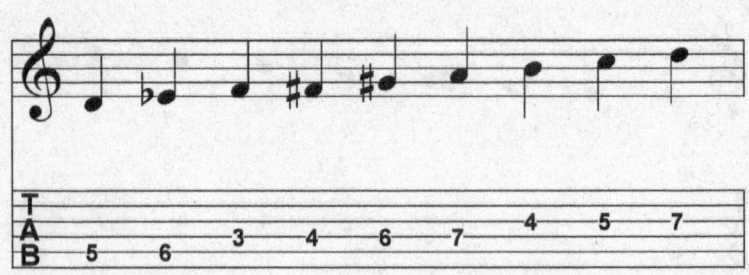

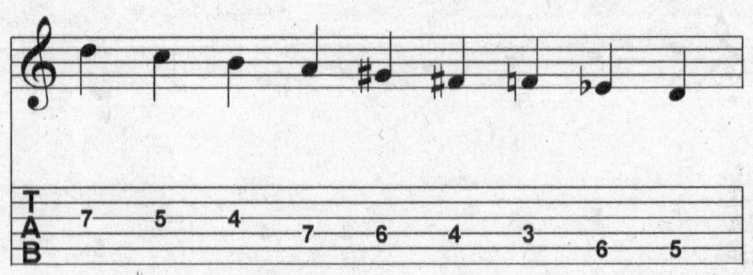

| Scale pattern | D E♭ F F♯ G♯ A B C D |
| | D C B A G♯ F♯ F♮ E♭ D |

D
Chromatic

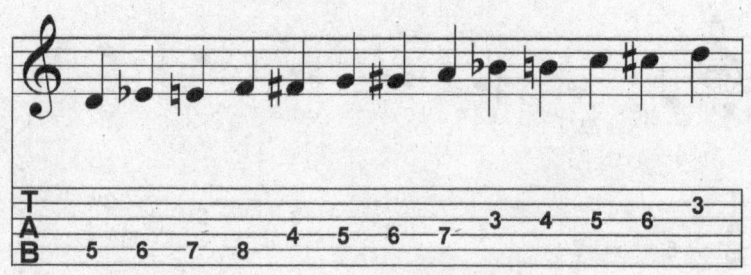

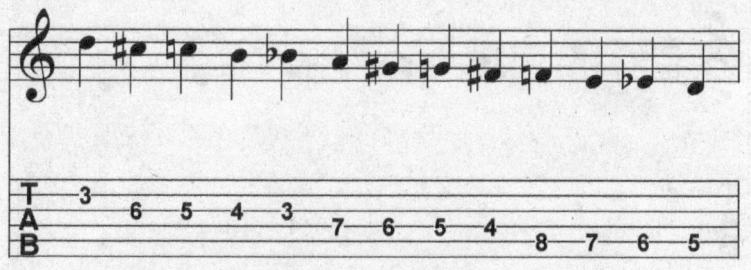

Scale pattern	D E♭ E♮ F F♯ G G♯ A B♭ B♮ C C♯ D
	D C♯ C♮ B B♭ A G♯ G♮ F♯ F♮ E E♭ D

Scan the code
to hear the chord

D
Wholetone

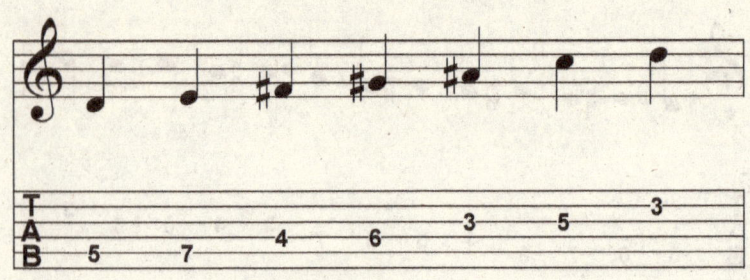

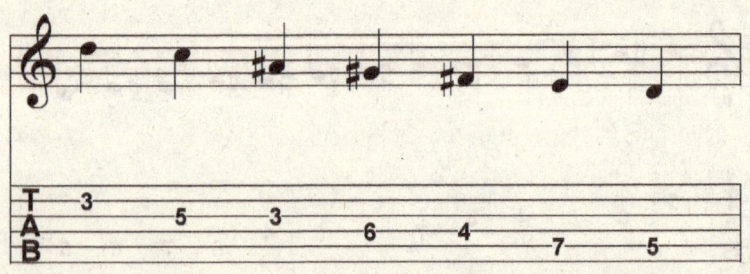

Scale pattern

D E F# G# A# C D
D C A# G# F# E D

Online access
flametreemusic.com

Scan the code
to hear the chord

134

D
Neapolitan

Scale pattern	D E♭ F G A B C♯ D
	D C♯ B A G F E♭ D

Online access
flametreemusic.com

Scan the code
to hear the chord

D#/E♭
Major (Ionian Mode)

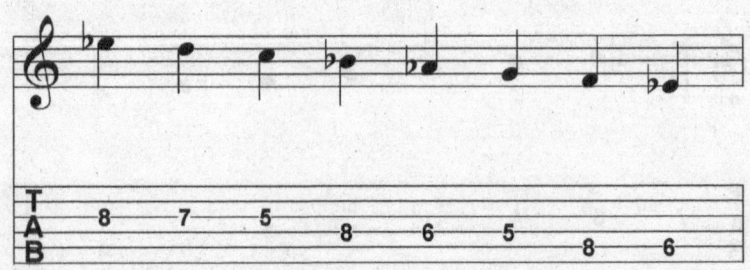

Scale pattern

E♭ F G A♭ B♭ C D E♭
E♭ D C B♭ A♭ G F E♭

D♯/E♭
Major Pentatonic

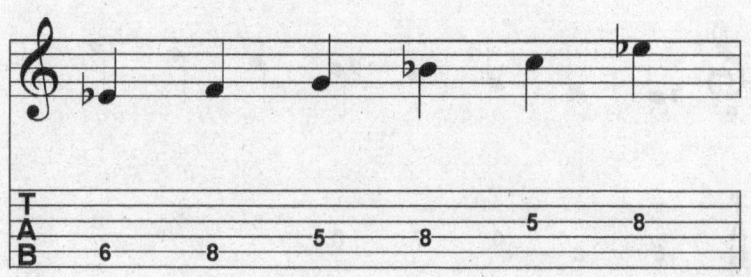

Scale pattern	E♭ F G B♭ C E♭
	E♭ C B♭ G F E♭

D♯/E♭
Lydian

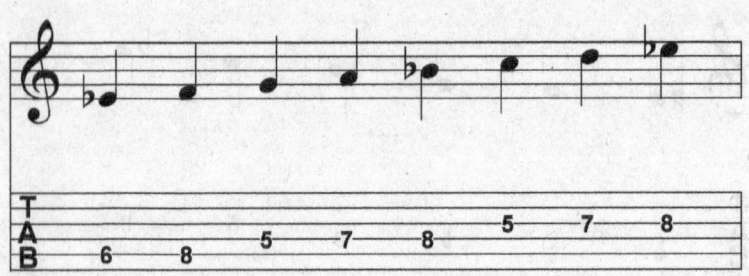

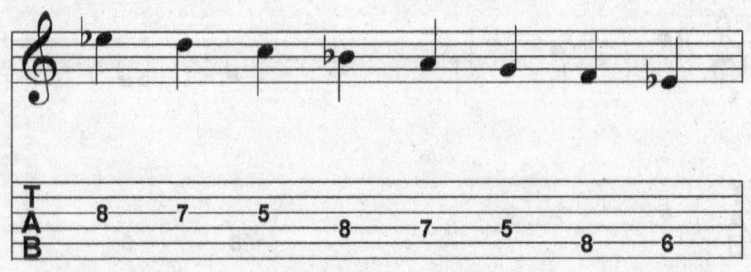

| **Scale pattern** | E♭ F G A B♭ C D E♭
E♭ D C B♭ A G F E♭ |

D♯/E♭
Lydian Augmented

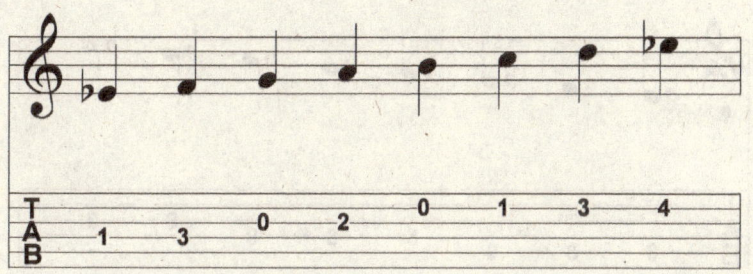

Scale pattern	E♭ F G A B C D E♭
	E♭ D C B A G F E♭

D♯/E♭
Natural Minor (Aeolian Mode)

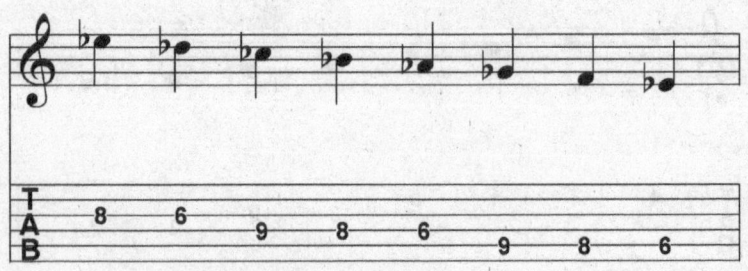

| **Scale pattern** | E♭ F G♭ A♭ B♭ C♭ D♭ E♭ |
| | E♭ D♭ C♭ B♭ A♭ G♭ F E♭ |

D#/E♭
Harmonic Minor

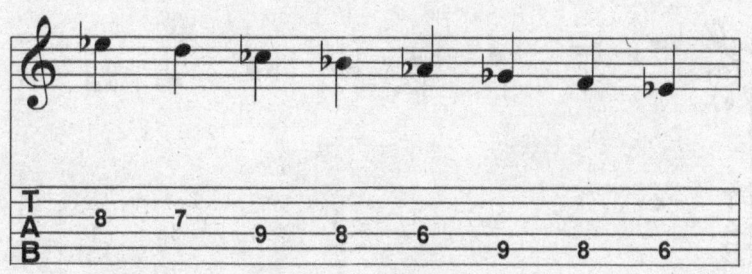

Scale pattern

E♭ F G♭ A♭ B♭ C♭ D E♭
E♭ D C♭ B♭ A♭ G♭ F E♭

D♯/E♭
Melodic Minor

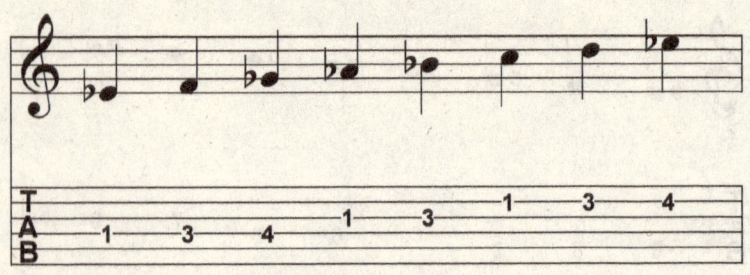

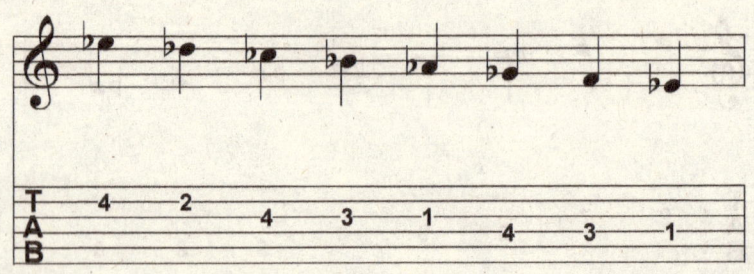

Scale pattern	E♭ F G♭ A♭ B♭ C D E♭
	E♭ D♭ C♭ B♭ A♭ G♭ F E♭

Online access
flametreemusic.com

Scan the code
to hear the chord

D♯/E♭
Dorian Mode

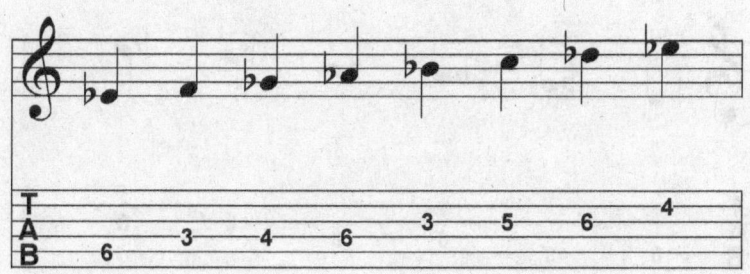

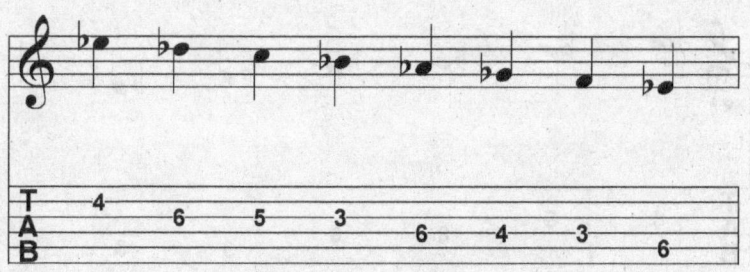

Scale pattern	E♭ F G♭ A♭ B♭ C D♭ E♭
	E♭ D♭ C B♭ A♭ G♭ F E♭

D#/E♭
Minor Pentatonic

Scale pattern

E♭ G♭ A♭ B♭ D♭ E♭
E♭ D♭ B♭ A♭ G♭ E♭

Online access
flametreemusic.com

Scan the code
to hear the chord

D#/E♭
Blues

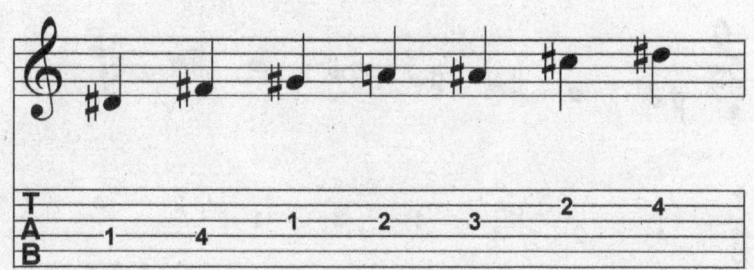

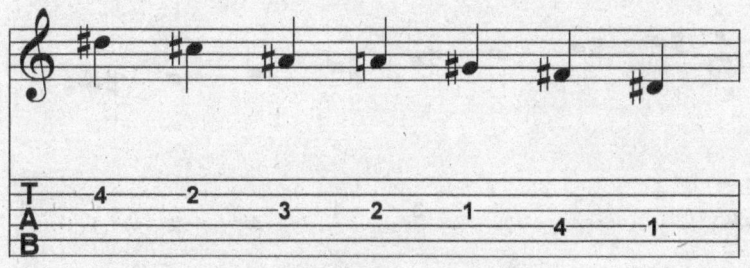

Scale pattern	D# F# G# A♮ A# C# D#
	D# C# A# A♮ G# F# D#

Online access
flametreemusic.com Scan the code
to hear the chord

D♯/E♭
Phrygian Mode

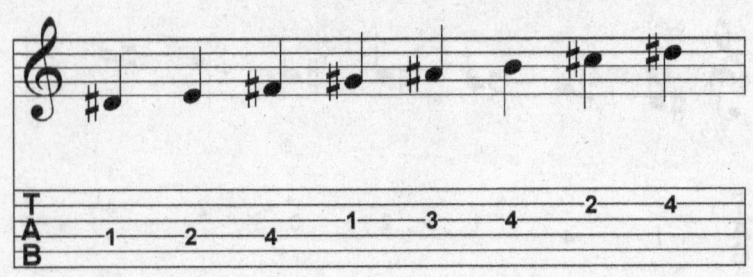

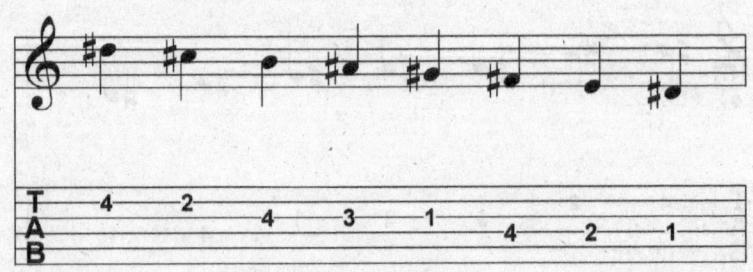

Scale pattern	D♯ E F♯ G♯ A♯ B C♯ D♯
	D♯ C♯ B A♯ G♯ F♯ E D♯

D♯/E♭
Locrian Mode

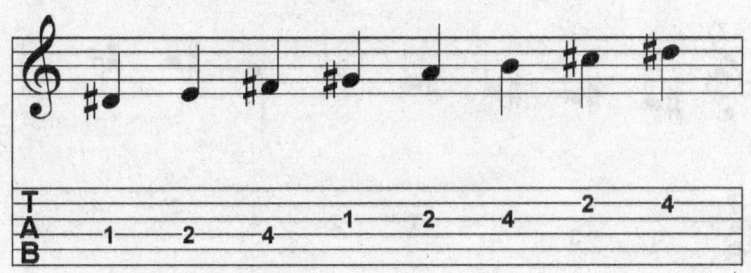

Scale pattern	D♯ E F♯ G♯ A B C♯ D♯
	D♯ C♯ B A G♯ F♯ E D♯

D♯/E♭
Half-diminished

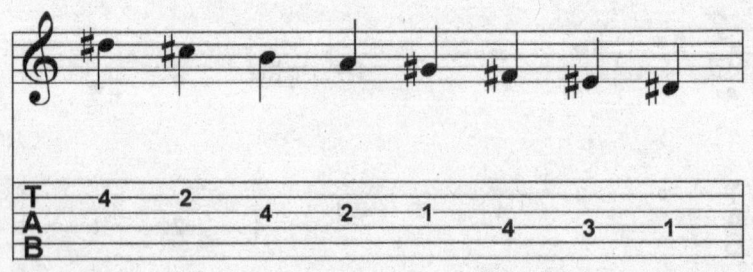

Scale pattern	D♯ E♯ F♯ G♯ A B C♯ D♯
	D♯ C♯ B A G♯ F♯ E♯ D♯

D♯/E♭
Mixolydian Mode

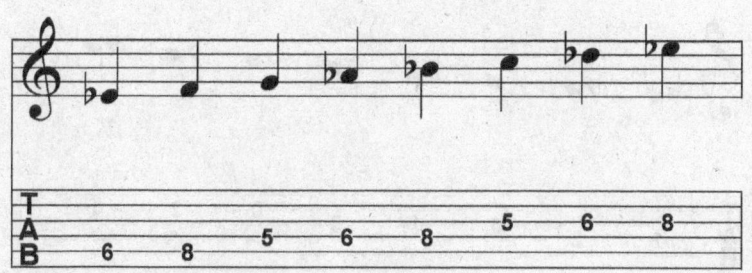

Scale pattern

E♭ F G A♭ B♭ C D♭ E♭
E♭ D♭ C B♭ A♭ G F E♭

D♯/E♭
Phrygian Major/Spanish

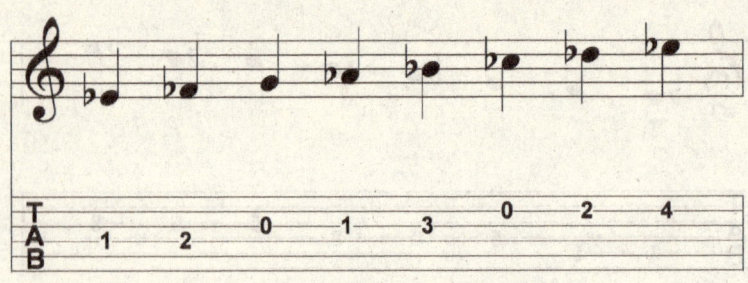

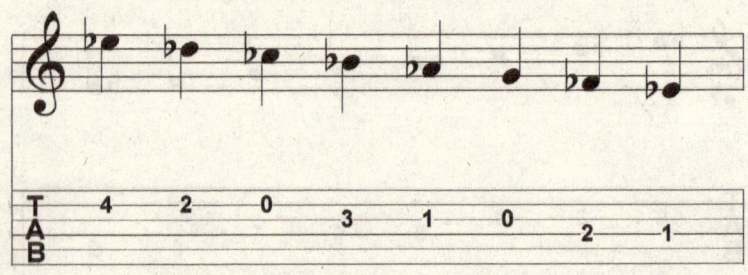

Scale pattern	E♭ F♭ G A♭ B♭ C♭ D♭ E♭
	E♭ D♭ C♭ B♭ A♭ G F♭ E♭

D♯/E♭
Lydian Dominant

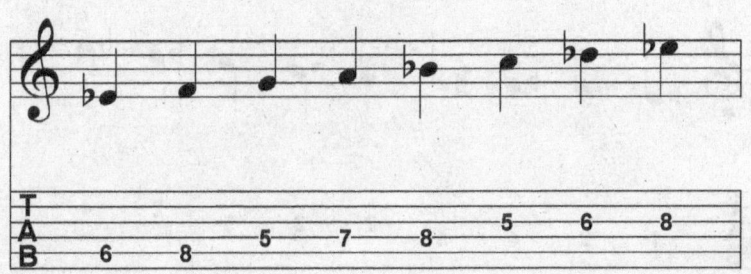

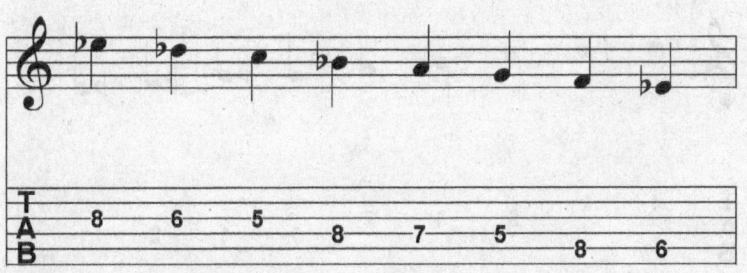

Scale pattern	E♭ F G A B♭ C D♭ E♭
	E♭ D♭ C B♭ A G F E♭

D♯/E♭
Diminished

Scale pattern	E♭ F♭ G♭ G♮ A B♭ C D♭ E♭
	E♭ D♭ C B♭ A G G♭ F♭ E♭

D♯/E♭
Chromatic

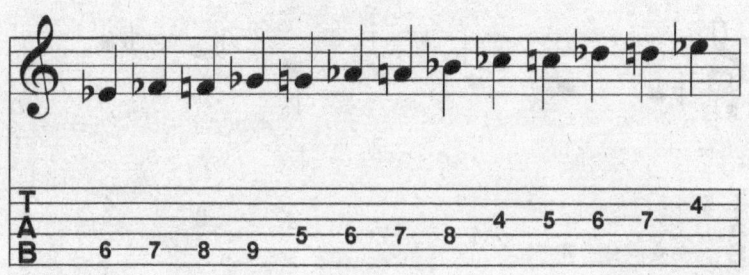

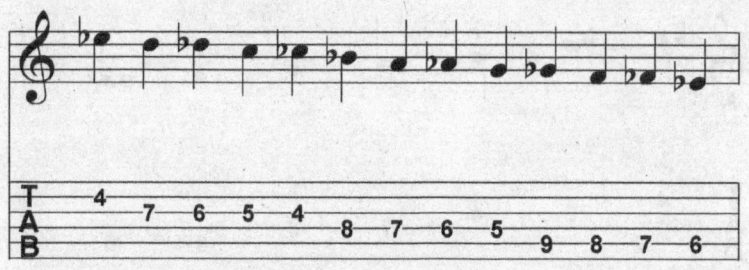

Scale pattern

E♭ F♭ F♮ G♭ G♮ A♭ A♮ B♭ C♭ C♮ D♭ D♮ E♭
E♭ D D♭ C C♭ B♭ A A♭ G G♭ F F♭ E♭

D♯/E♭
Wholetone

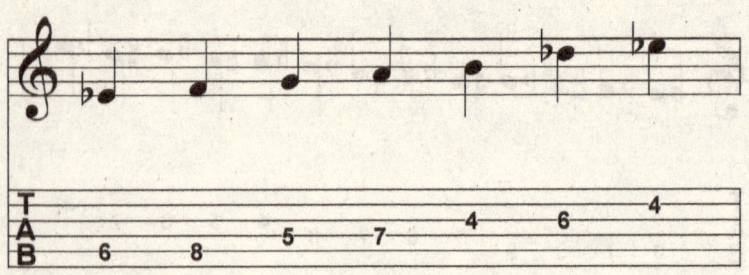

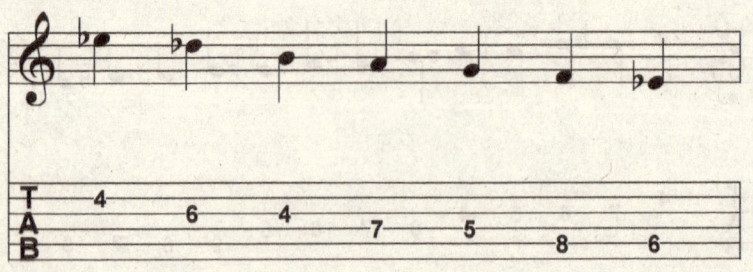

Scale pattern	E♭ F G A B D♭ E♭
	E♭ D♭ B A G F E♭

D#/E♭
Neapolitan

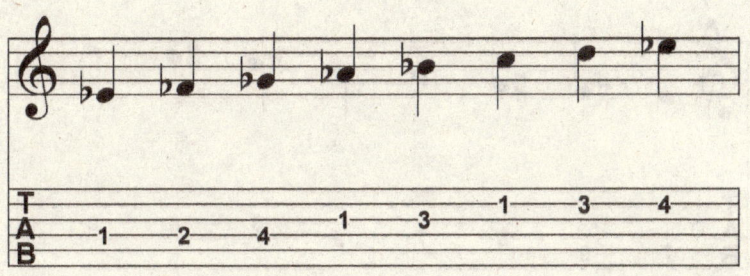

Scale pattern	E♭ F♭ G♭ A♭ B♭ C D E♭
	E♭ D C B♭ A♭ G♭ F♭ E♭

E
Major (Ionian Mode)

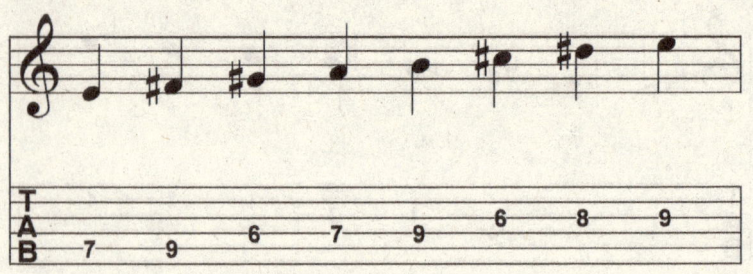

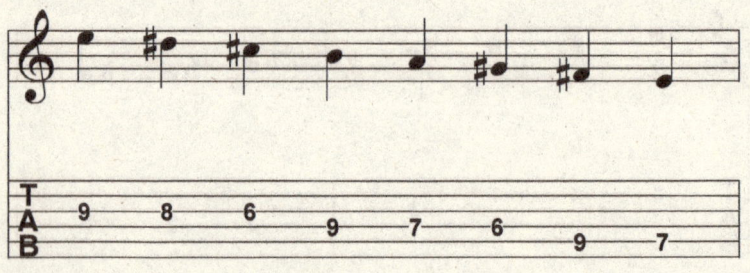

| **Scale pattern** | E F# G# A B C# D# E |
| | E D# C# B A G# F# E |

E
Major Pentatonic

Scale pattern	E F# G# B C# E
	E C# B G# F# E

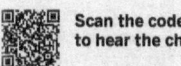

E
Lydian Mode

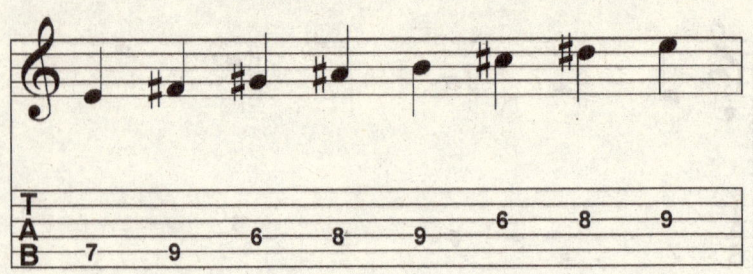

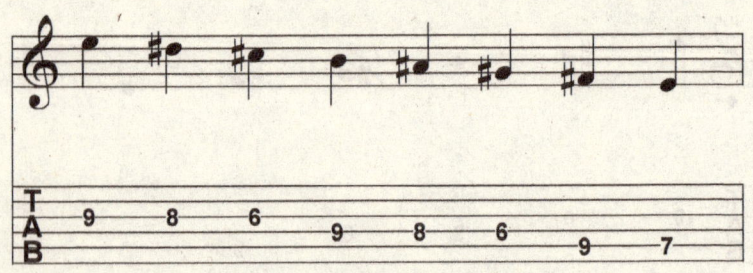

Scale pattern	E F# G# A# B C# D# E
	E D# C# B A# G# F# E

E
Lydian Augmented

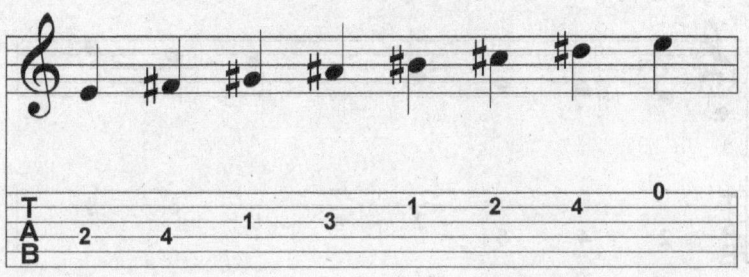

Scale pattern	E F# G# A# B# C# D# E
	E D# C# B# A# G# F# E

E

Natural Minor (Aeolian Mode)

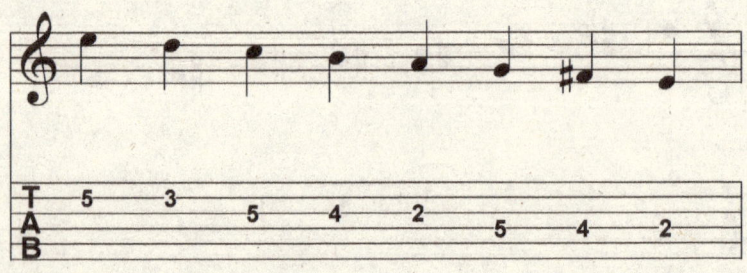

| Scale pattern | E F♯ G A B C D E |
| | E D C B A G F♯ E |

E
Harmonic Minor

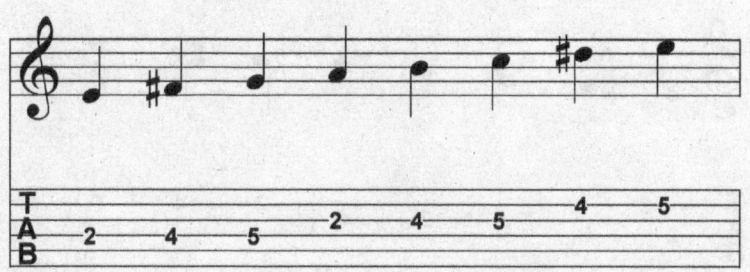

Scale pattern	E F♯ G A B C D♯ E
	E D♯ C B A G F♯ E

E
Melodic Minor

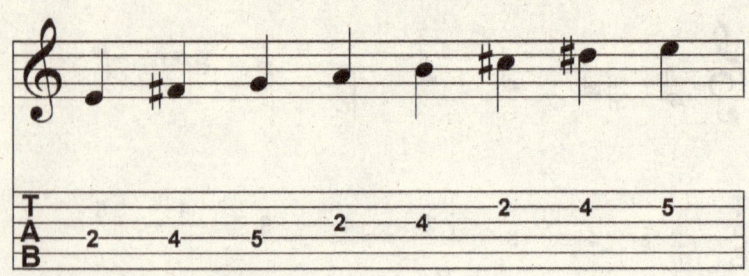

| Scale pattern | E F♯ G A B C♯ D♯ E |
| | E D♮ C♮ B A G F♯ E |

E
Dorian Mode

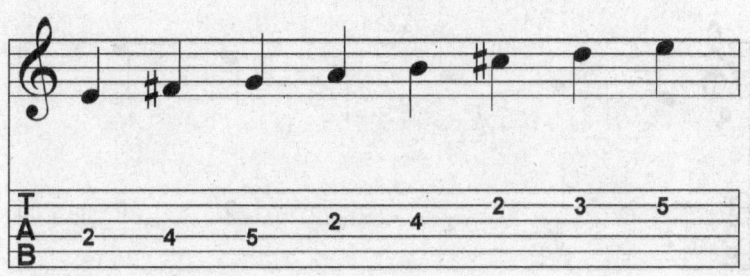

Scale pattern	E F♯ G A B C♯ D E
	E D C♯ B A G F♯ E

E
Minor Pentatonic

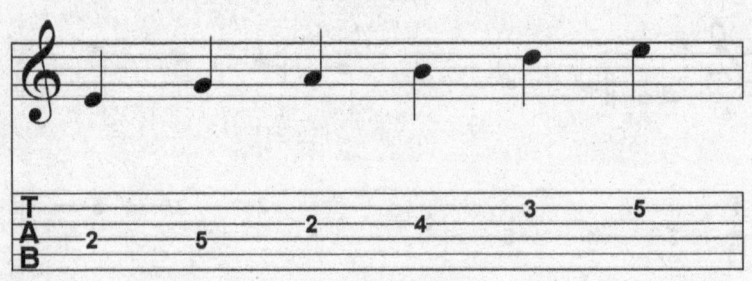

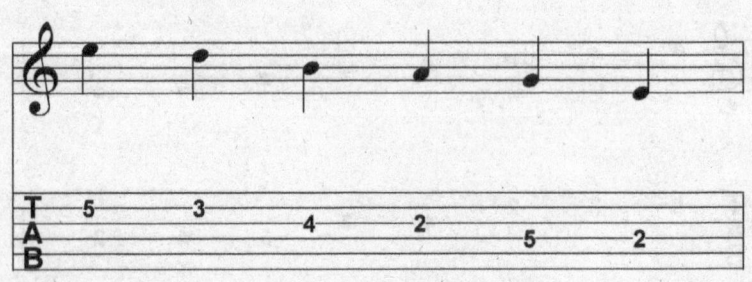

Scale pattern

E G A B D E
E D B A G E

E
Blues

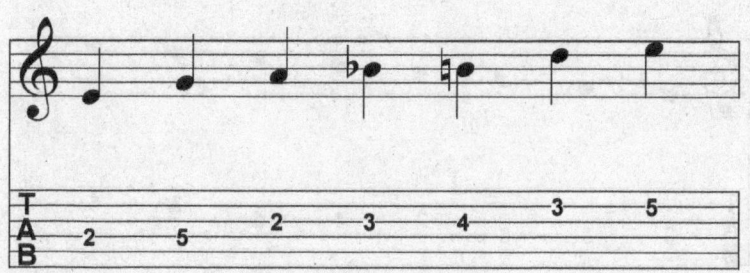

| Scale pattern | E G A B♭ B♮ D E |
| | E D B♮ B♭ A G E |

E
Phrygian Mode

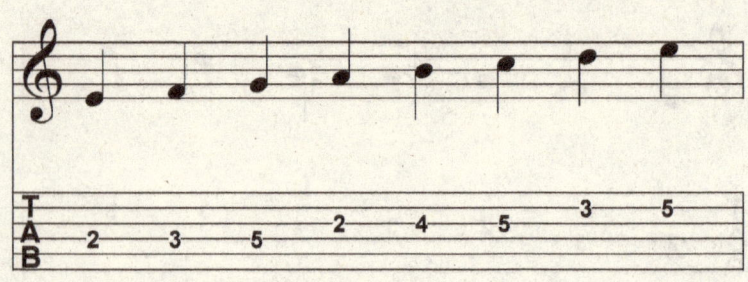

Scale pattern	E F G A B C D E
	E D C B A G F E

E
Locrian Mode

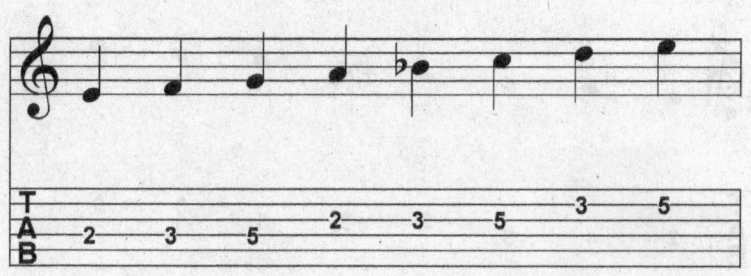

Scale pattern	E F G A B♭ C D E
	E D C B♭ A G F E

Online access
flametreemusic.com

Scan the code
to hear the chord

E
Half-diminished

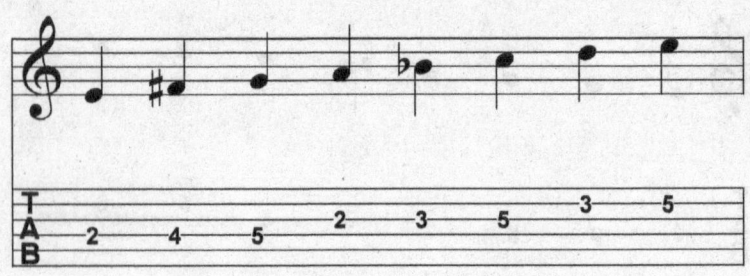

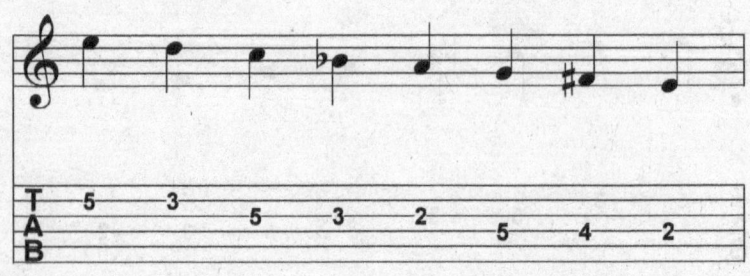

Scale pattern	E F♯ G A B♭ C D E
	E D C B♭ A G F♯ E

E
Mixolydian Mode

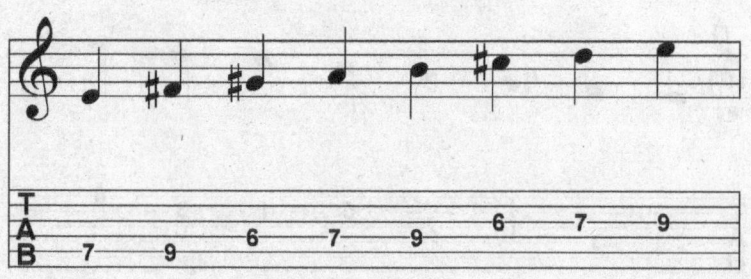

| **Scale pattern** | E F# G# A B C# D E |
| | E D C# B A G# F# E |

E
Phrygian Major/Spanish

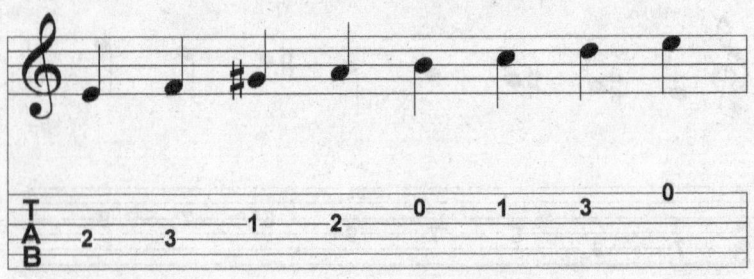

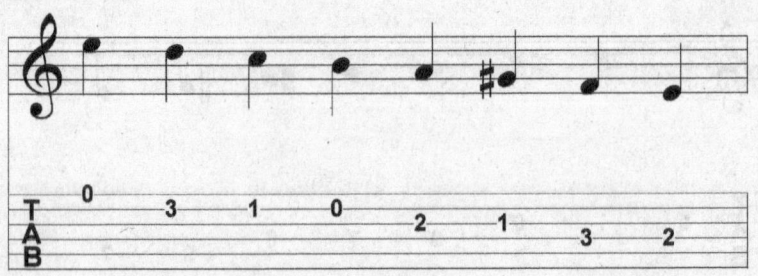

Scale pattern	E F G♯ A B C D E
	E D C B A G♯ F E

E
Lydian Dominant

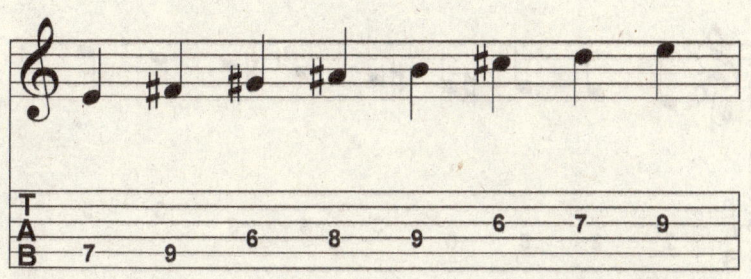

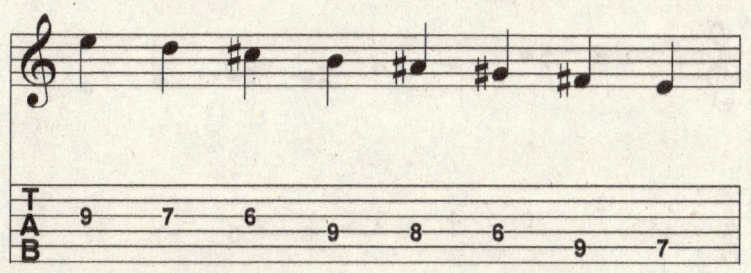

Scale pattern	E F♯ G♯ A♯ B C♯ D E
	E D C♯ B A♯ G♯ F♯ E

E
Diminished

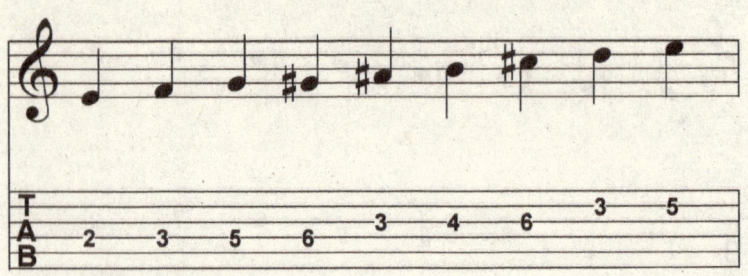

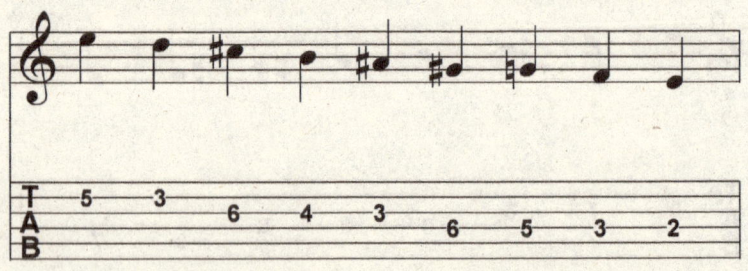

Scale pattern	E F G G# A# B C# D E
	E D C# B A# G# G♮ F E

E
Chromatic

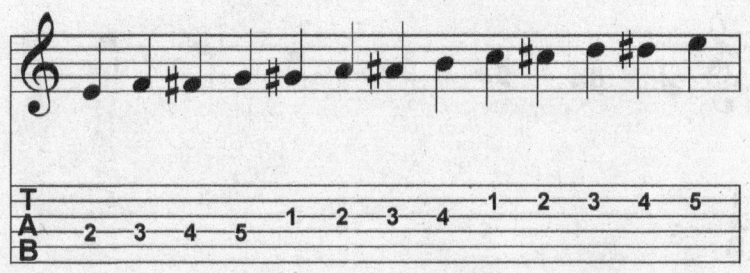

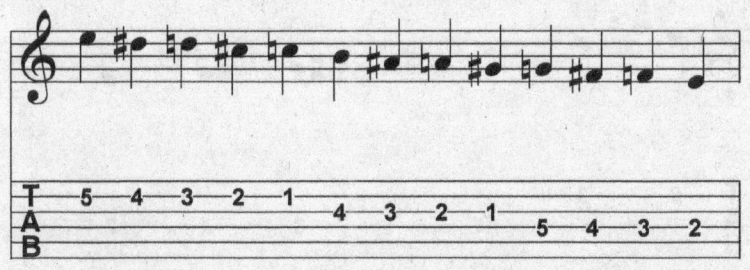

| Scale pattern | E F F# G G# A A# B C C# D D# E |
| | E D# D♮ C# C♮ B A# A♮ G# G♮ F# F♮ E |

E
Wholetone

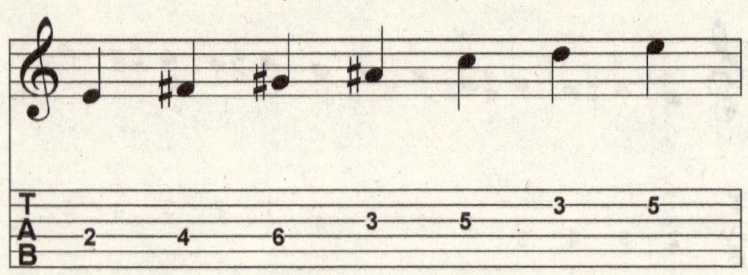

Scale pattern	E F# G# A# C D E
	E D C A# G# F# E

Online access
flametreemusic.com

Scan the code
to hear the chord

E
Neapolitan

| **Scale pattern** | E F G A B C♯ D♯ E |
| | E D♯ C♯ B A G F E |

F
Major (Ionian Mode)

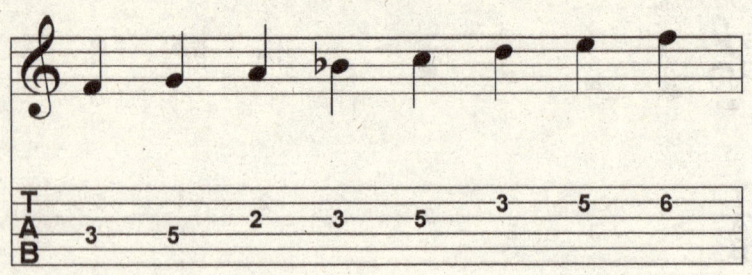

Scale pattern	F G A B♭ C D E F
	F E D C B♭ A G F

F
Major Pentatonic

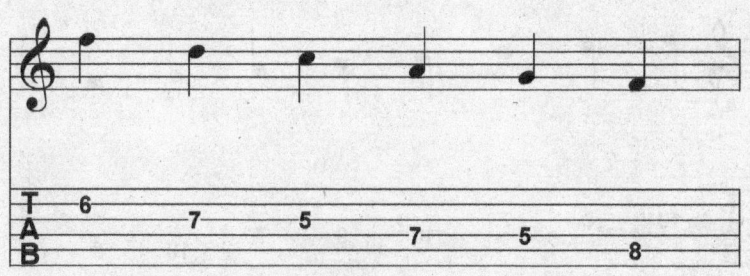

Scale pattern	F G A C D F F D C A G F

F
Lydian Mode

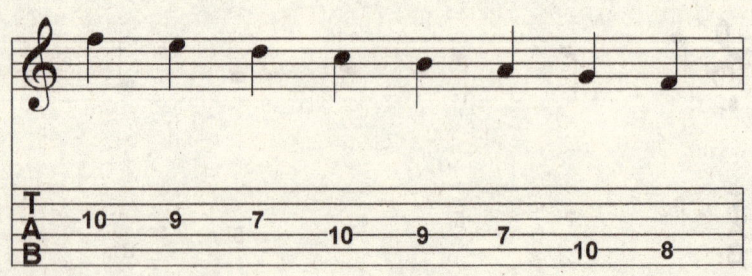

| **Scale pattern** | F G A B C D E F |
| | F E D C B A G F |

F
Lydian Augmented

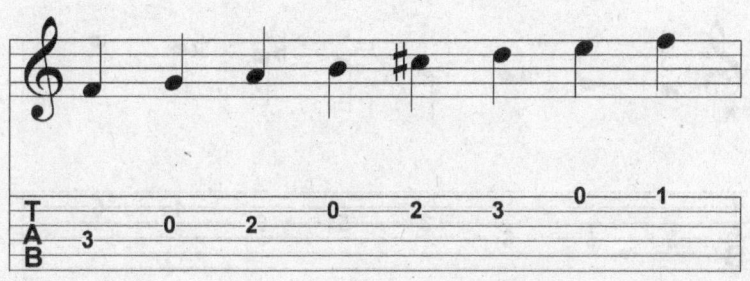

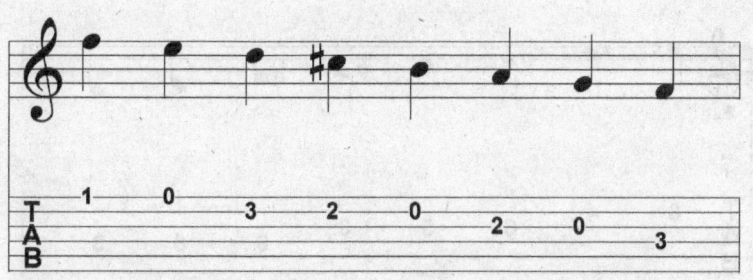

| Scale pattern | F G A B C# D E F |
| | F E D C# B A G F |

F
Natural Minor (Aeolian Mode)

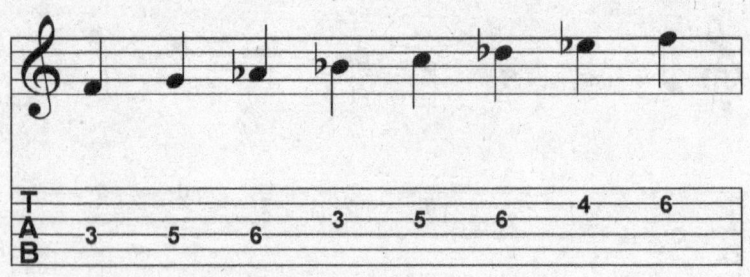

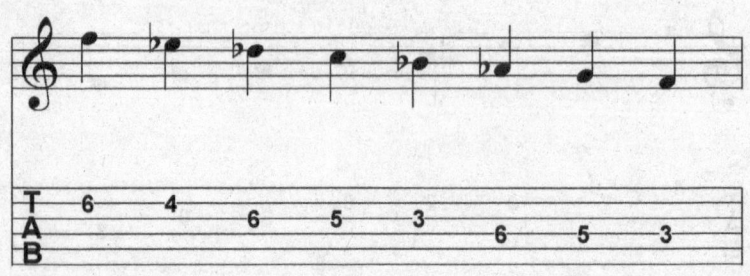

Scale pattern	F G A♭ B♭ C D♭ E♭ F
	F E♭ D♭ C B♭ A♭ G F

F
Harmonic Minor

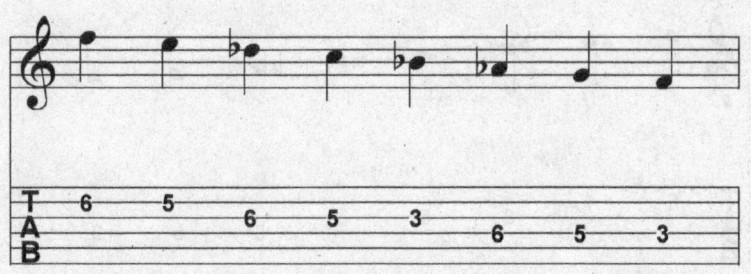

Scale pattern	F G A♭ B♭ C D♭ E F
	F E D♭ C B♭ A♭ G F

F
Melodic Minor

| Scale pattern | F G A♭ B♭ C D E F |
| | F E♭ D♭ C B♭ A♭ G F |

Online access
flametreemusic.com

Scan the code
to hear the chord

F
Dorian Mode

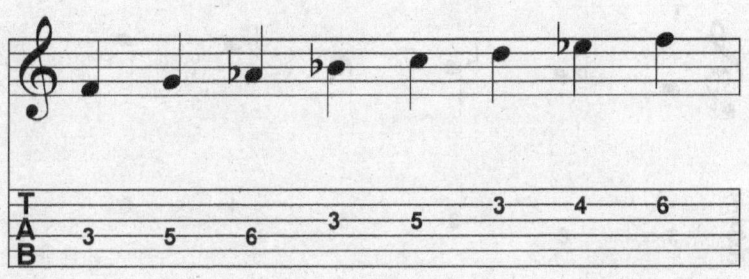

Scale pattern	F G A♭ B♭ C D E♭ F
	F E♭ D C B♭ A♭ G F

F
Minor Pentatonic

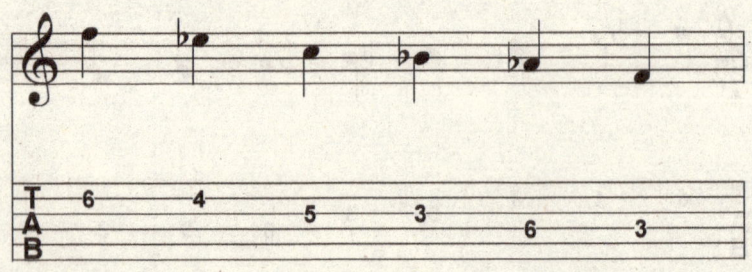

| **Scale pattern** | F A♭ B♭ C E♭ F |
| | F E♭ C B♭ A♭ F |

F
Blues

Scale pattern	F A♭ B♭ C♭ C♮ E♭ F
	F E♭ C♮ C♭ B♭ A♭ F

F
Phrygian Mode

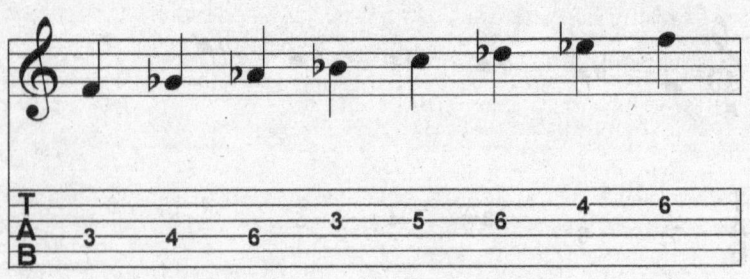

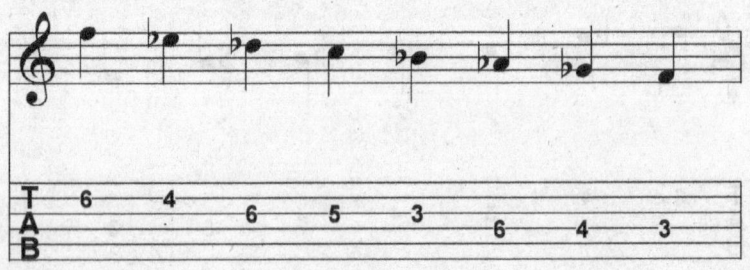

Scale pattern

F G♭ A♭ B♭ C D♭ E♭ F
F E♭ D♭ C B♭ A♭ G♭ F

F
Locrian Mode

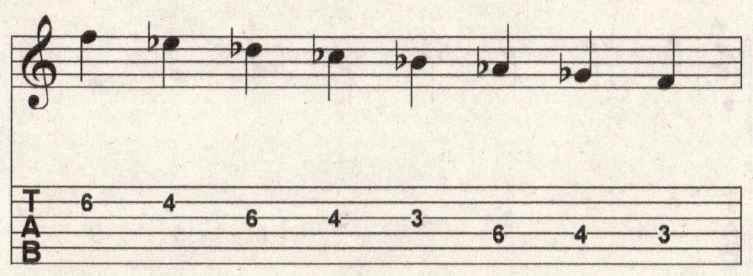

Scale pattern	F G♭ A♭ B♭ C♭ D♭ E♭ F
	F E♭ D♭ C♭ B♭ A♭ G♭ F

F
Half-diminished

Scale pattern

F G A♭ B♭ C♭ D♭ E♭ F
F E♭ D♭ C♭ B♭ A♭ G F

F
Mixolydian Mode

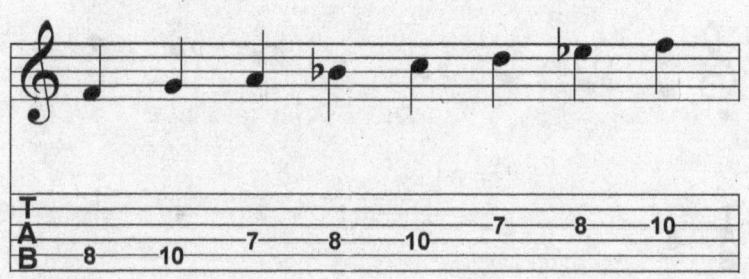

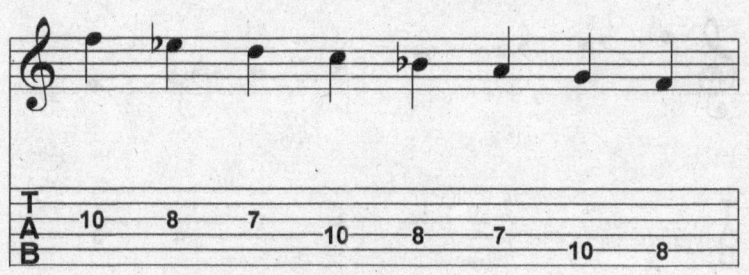

Scale pattern	F G A B♭ C D E♭ F F E♭ D C B♭ A G F

F
Phrygian Major/Spanish

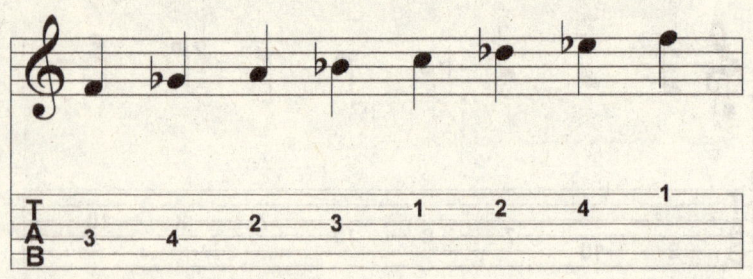

Scale pattern	F G♭ A B♭ C D♭ E♭ F
	F E♭ D♭ C B♭ A G♭ F

Online access
flametreemusic.com

Scan the code
to hear the chord

F
Lydian Dominant

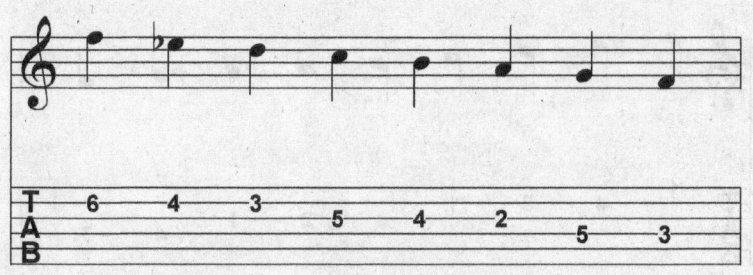

Scale pattern	F G A B C D♭ F
	F♭ D C B A G F

Online access
flametreemusic.com

Scan the code
to hear the chord

191

F
Diminished

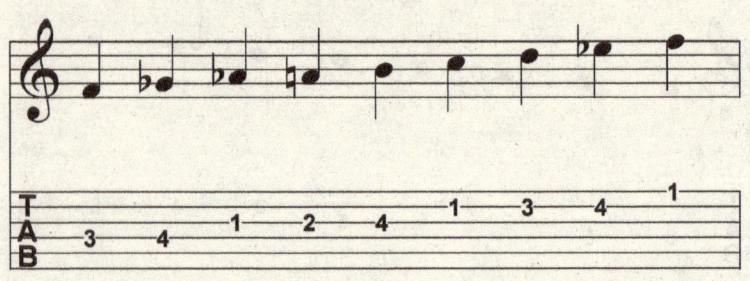

Scale pattern	F G♭ A♭ A♮ B C D E♭ F
	F E♭ D C B A A♭ G♭ F

F
Chromatic

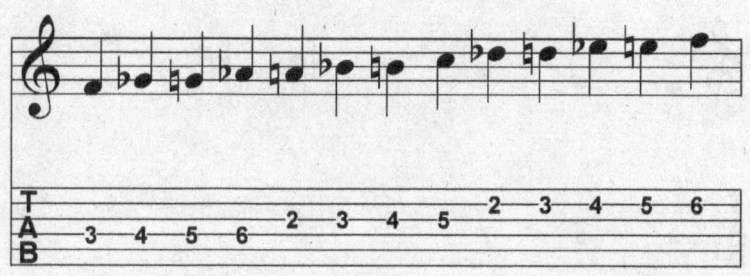

Scale pattern

F. Gb G♮ Ab A♮ Bb B♮ C Db D♮ Eb E♮ F
F E E♭ D D♭ C B B♭ A A♭ G G♭ F

F
Wholetone

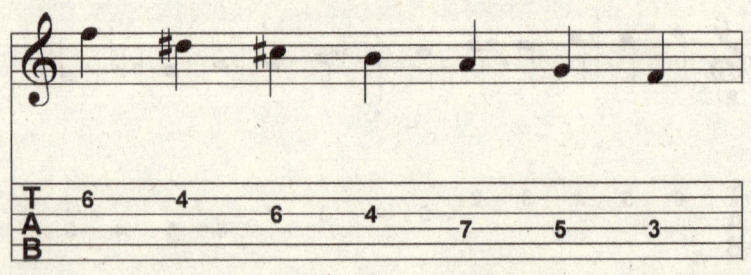

Scale pattern

F G A B C♯ D♯ F
F D♯ C♯ B A G F

F
Neapolitan

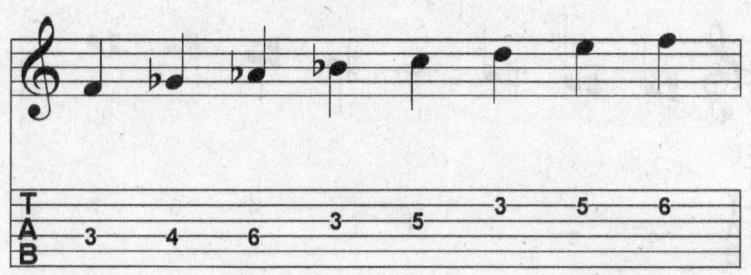

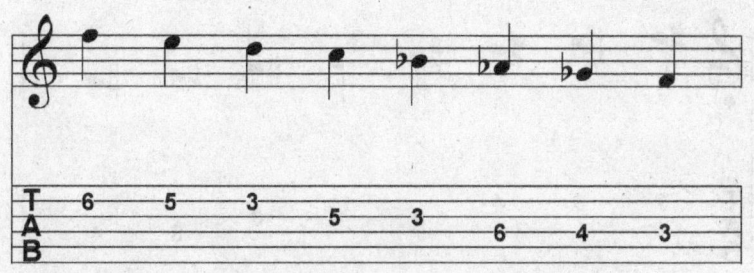

| **Scale pattern** | F G♭ A♭ B♭ C D E F |
| | F E D C B♭ A♭ G♭ F |

F#/Gb
Major (Ionian Mode)

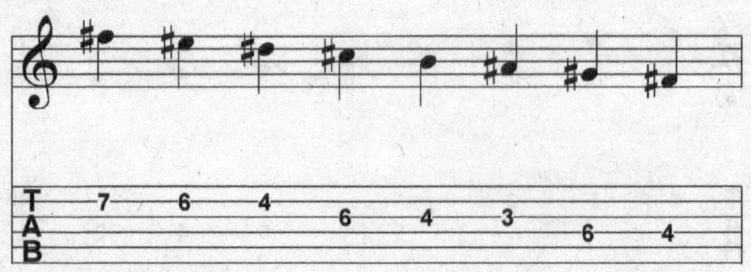

Scale pattern

F# G# A# B C# D# E# F#
F# E# D# C# B A# G# F#

F♯/G♭
Major Pentatonic

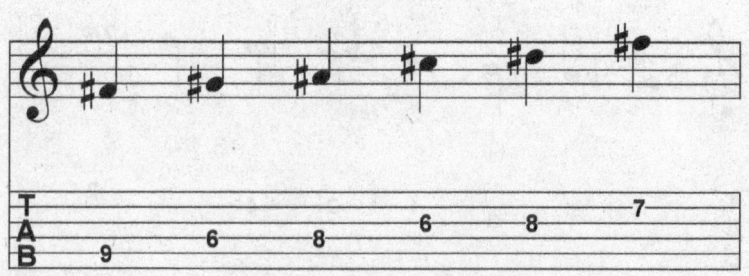

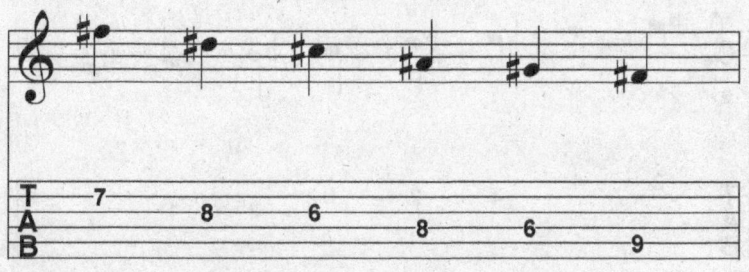

Scale pattern	F♯ G♯ A♯ C♯ D♯ F♯
	F♯ D♯ C♯ A♯ G♯ F♯

F#/G♭
Lydian Mode

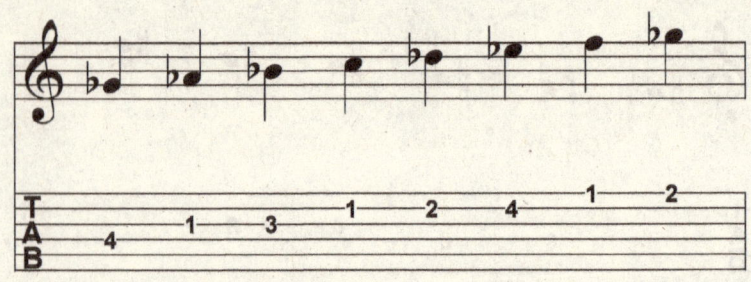

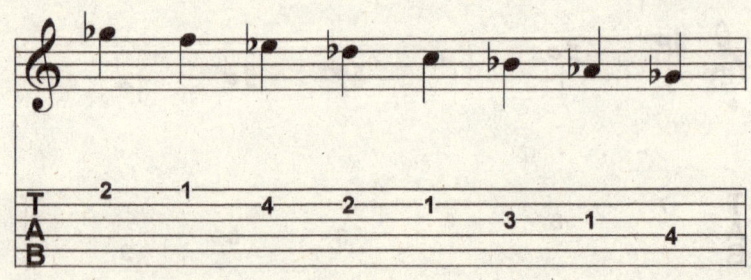

Scale pattern

G♭ A♭ B♭ C D♭ E♭ F G♭

G♭ F E♭ D♭ C B♭ A♭ G♭

F♯/G♭
Lydian Augmented

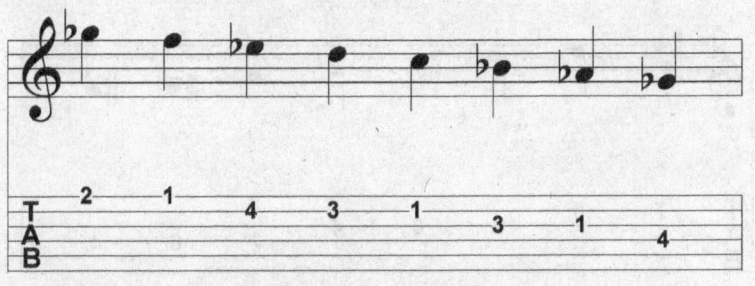

Scale pattern	G♭ A♭ B♭ C D E♭ F G♭
	G♭ F E♭ D C B♭ A♭ G♭

F#/Gb
Natural Minor (Aeolian Mode)

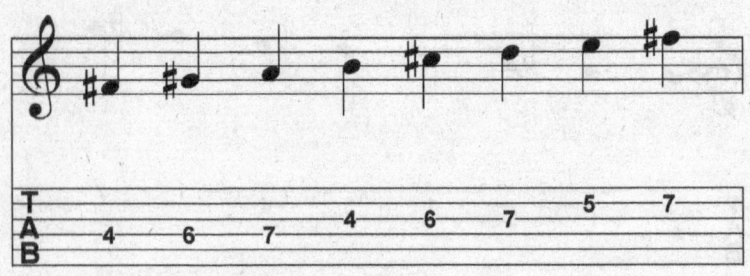

Scale pattern	F# G# A B C# D E F#
	F# E D C# B A G# F#

F♯/G♭
Harmonic Minor

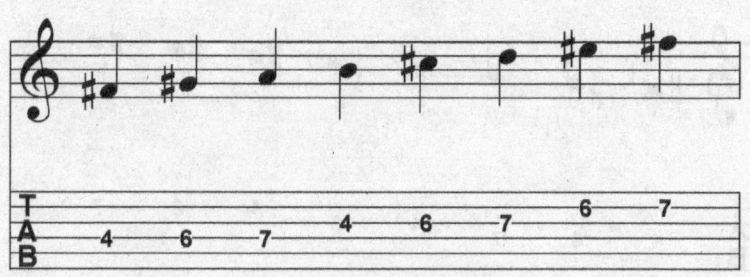

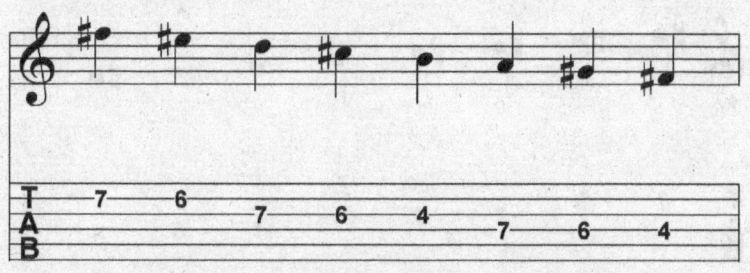

| Scale pattern | F♯ G♯ A B C♯ D E♯ F♯ |
| | F♯ E♯ D C♯ B A G♯ F♯ |

F♯/G♭
Melodic Minor

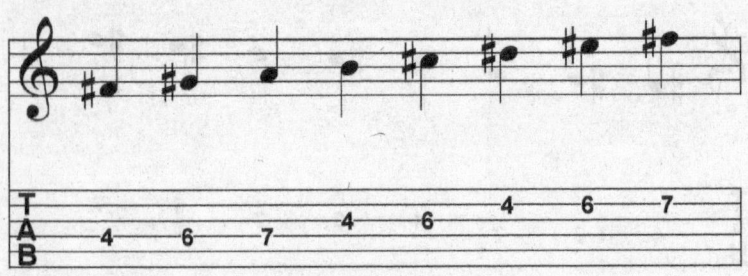

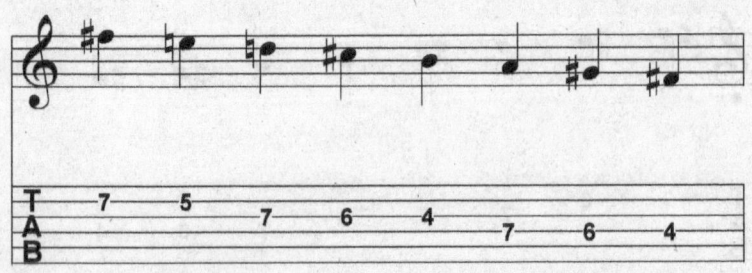

Scale pattern

F♯ G♯ A B C♯ D♯ E♯ F♯

F♯ E♮ D♮ C♯ B A G♯ F♯

F#/G♭
Dorian Mode

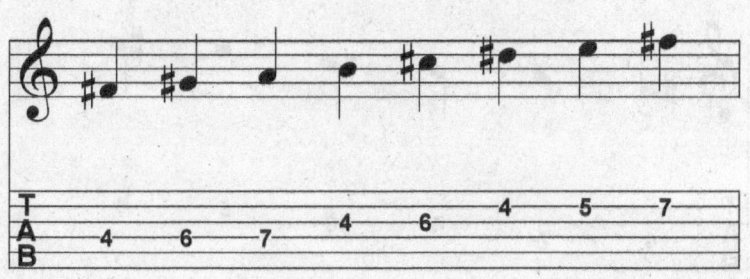

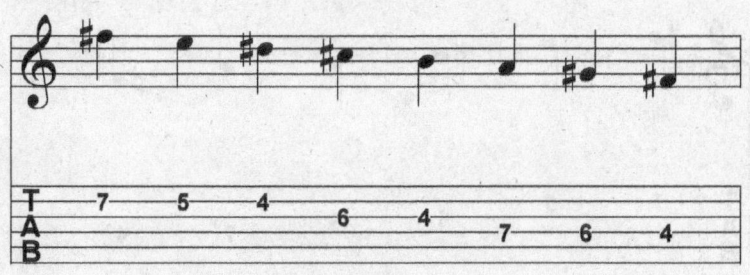

Scale pattern	F# G# A B C# D# E F#
	F# E D# C# B A G# F#

F♯/G♭
Minor Pentatonic

Scale pattern	F♯ A B C♯ E F♯ F♯ E C♯ B A F♯

F♯/G♭
Blues

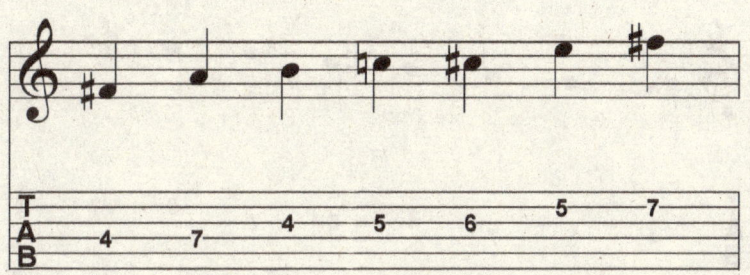

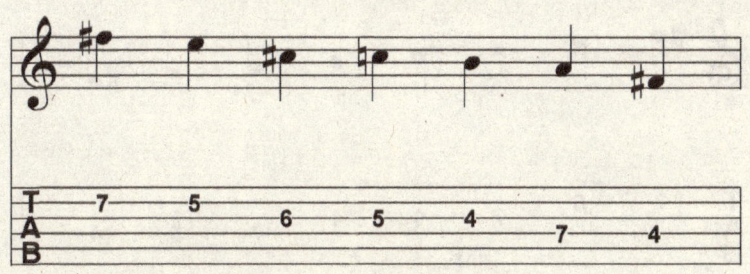

Scale pattern	F♯ A B C♮ C♯ E F♯
	F♯ E C♯ C♮ B A F♯

F♯/G♭
Phrygian Mode

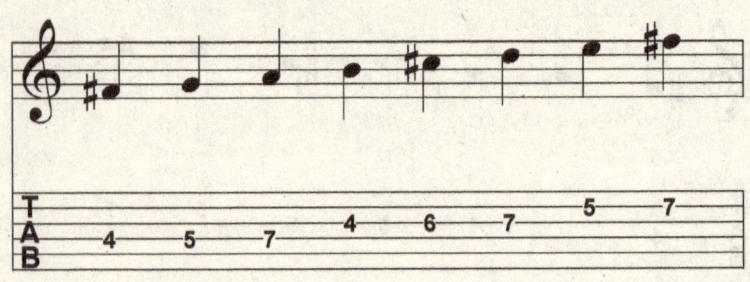

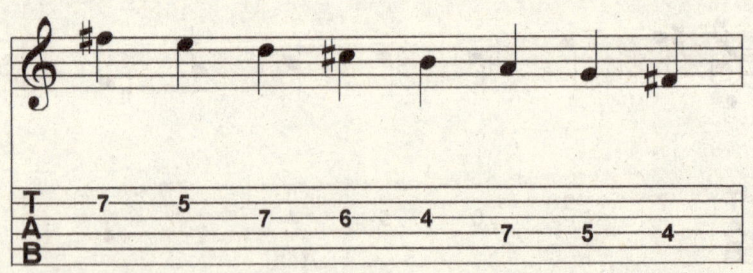

Scale pattern	F♯ G A B C♯ D E F♯
	F♯ E D C♯ B A G F♯

F♯/G♭
Locrian Mode

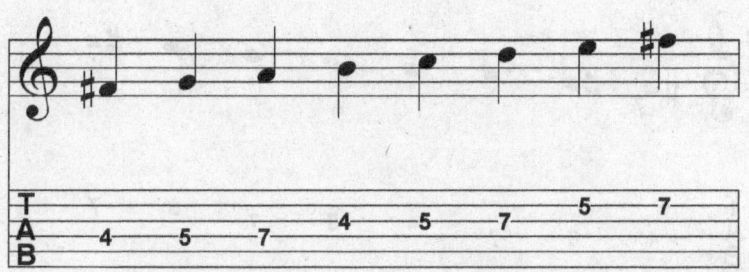

Scale pattern	F♯ G A B C D E F♯
	F♯ E D C B A G F♯

F#/G♭
Half-diminished

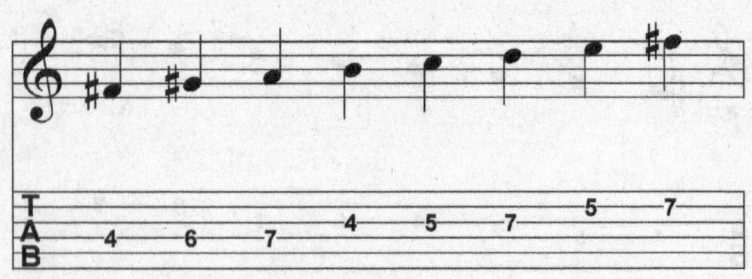

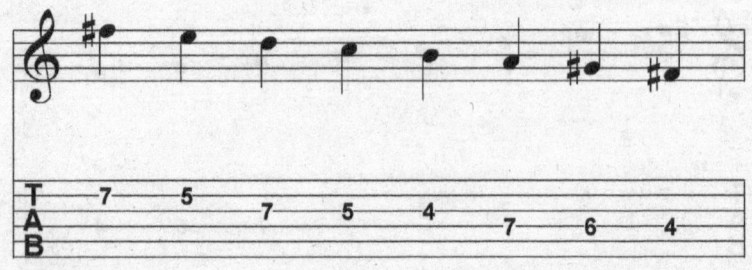

Scale pattern	F# G# A B C D E F#
	F# E D C B A G# F#

F♯/G♭
Mixolydian Mode

Scale pattern	F♯ G♯ A♯ B C♯ D♯ E F♯
	F♯ E D♯ C♯ B A♯ G♯ F♯

F#/G♭
Phrygian Major/Spanish

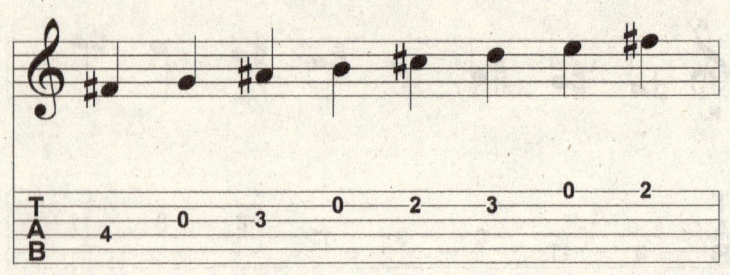

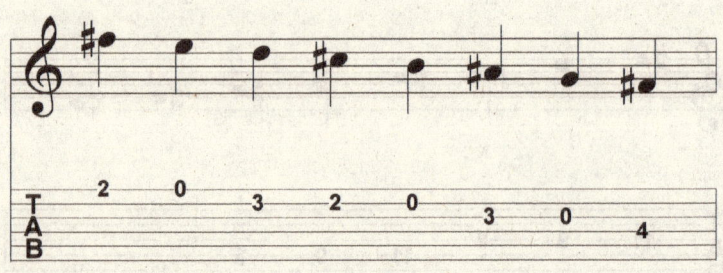

| **Scale pattern** | F# G A# B C# D E F# |
| | F# E D C# B A# G F# |

F♯/G♭
Lydian Dominant

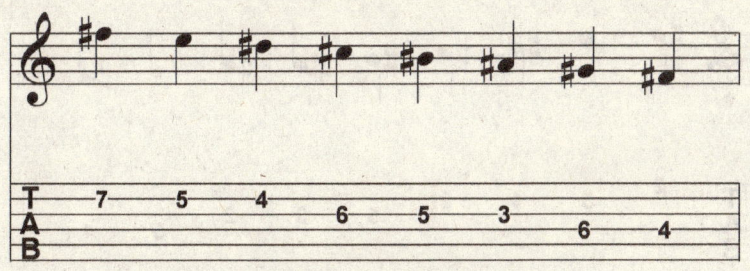

Scale pattern	F♯ G♯ A♯ B♯ C♯ D♯ E F♯
	F♯ E D♯ C♯ B♯ A♯ G♯ F♯

Online access
flametreemusic.com

Scan the code
to hear the chord

F#/Gb
Diminished

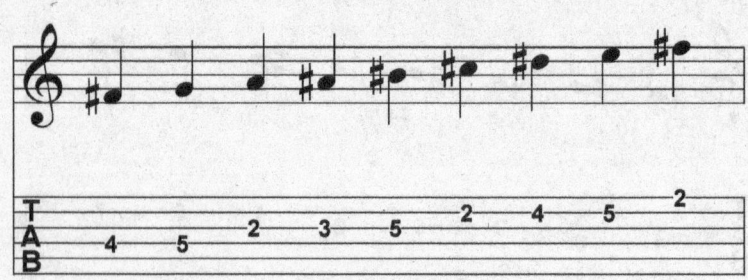

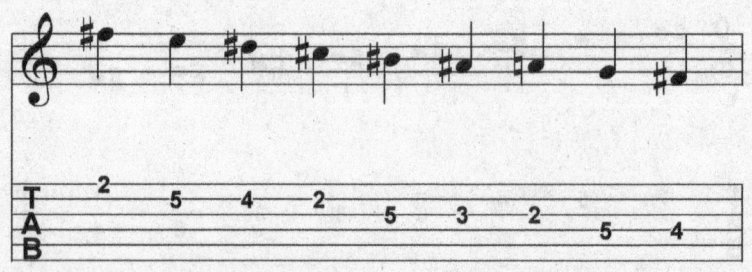

Scale pattern	F# G A A# B# C# D# E F#
	F# E D# C# B# A# A♮ G F#

F#/Gb
Chromatic

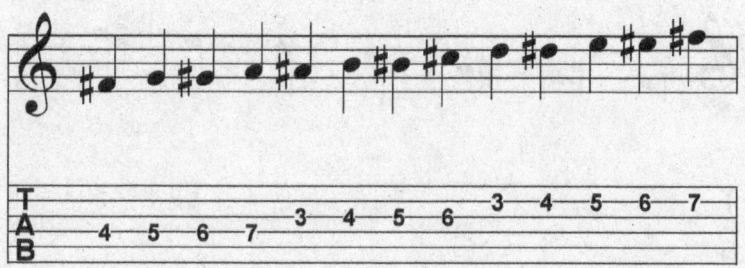

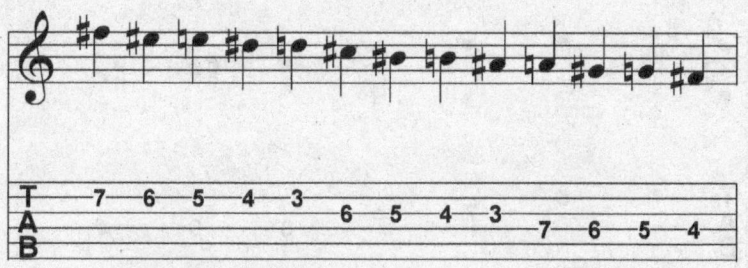

Scale pattern	F# G G# A A# B B# C# D D# E E# F#
	F# E# E♮ D# D♮ C# B# B♮ A# A♮ G# G♮ F#

F#/G♭
Wholetone

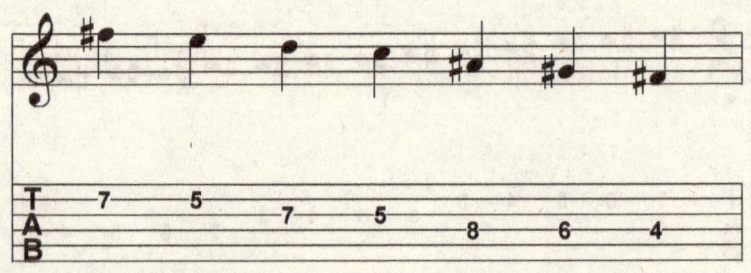

Scale pattern

F# G# A# C D E F#
F# E D C A# G# F#

F#/G♭
Neapolitan

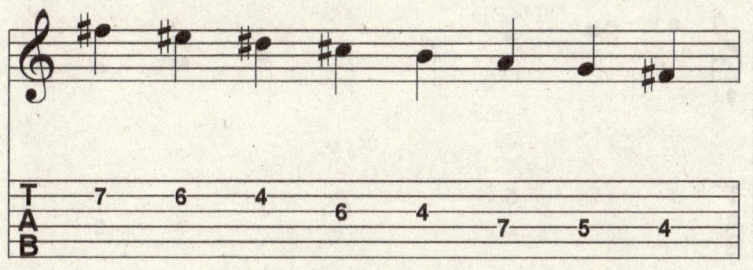

Scale pattern

F# G A B C# D# E# F#
F# E# D# C# B A G F#

G
Major (Ionian Mode)

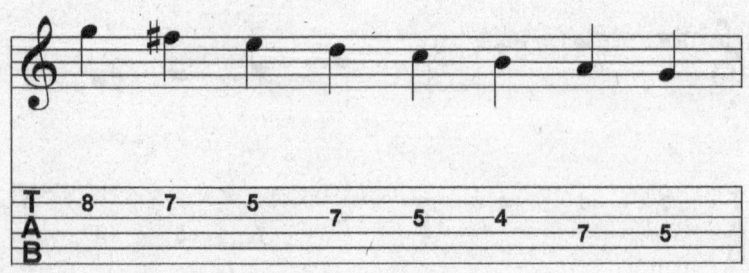

Scale pattern	G A B C D E F♯ G
	G F♯ E D C B A G

Online access
flametreemusic.com

Scan the code
to hear the chord

G
Major Pentatonic

Scale pattern	G A B D E G
	G E D B A G

G
Lydian Mode

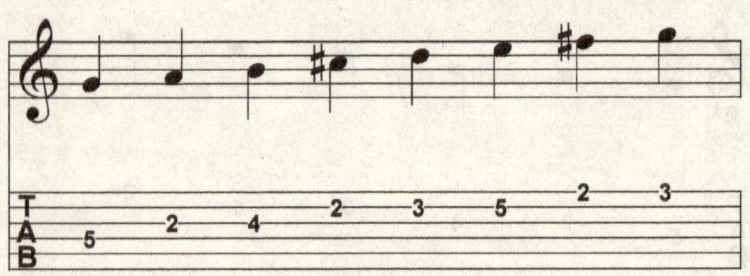

Scale pattern	G A B C♯ D E F♯ G
	G F♯ E D C♯ B A G

G
Lydian Augmented

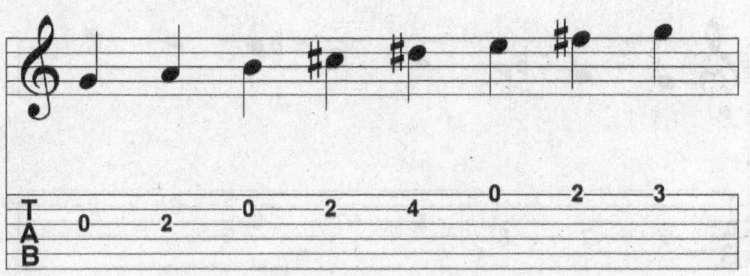

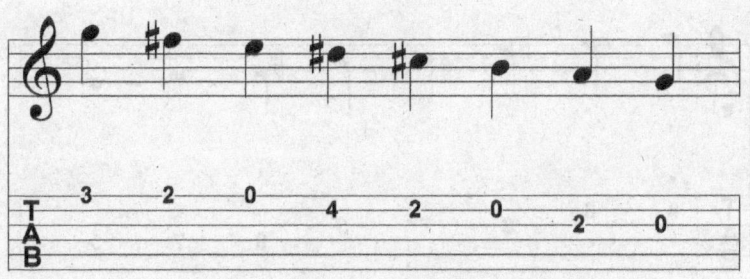

Scale pattern	G A B C♯ D♯ E F♯ G
	G F♯ E D♯ C♯ B A G

G
Natural Minor (Aeolian Mode)

Scale pattern	G A B♭ C D B♭ F G
	G F B♭ D C B♭ A G

G
Harmonic Minor

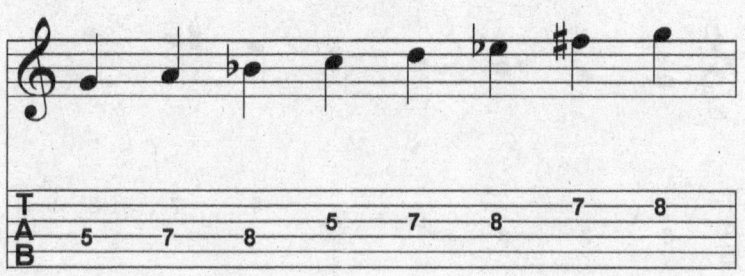

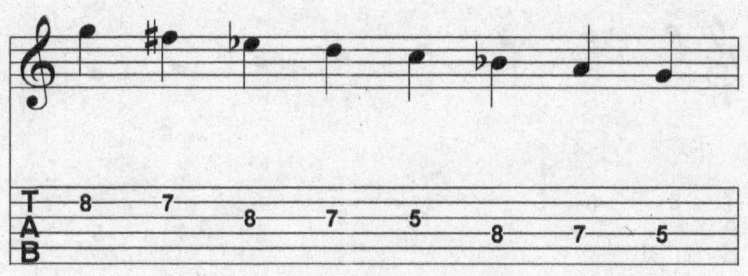

Scale pattern	G A B♭ C D E♭ F♯ G
	G F♯ E♭ D C B♭ A G

G
Melodic Minor

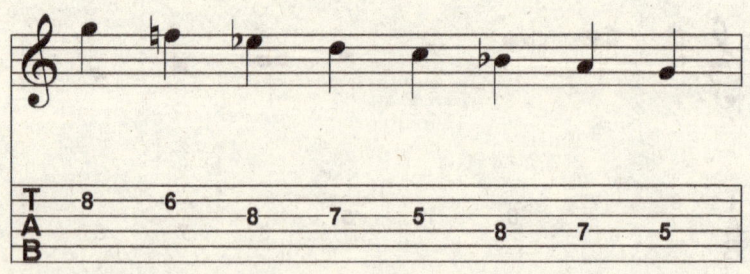

Scale pattern	G A B♭ C D E F♯ G
	G F♮ E♭ D C B♭ A G

Online access
flametreemusic.com

Scan the code
to hear the chord

G
Dorian Mode

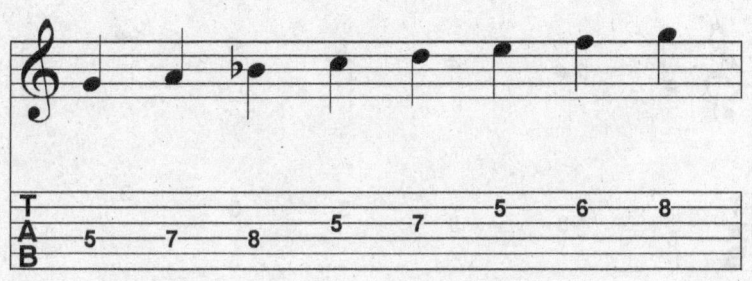

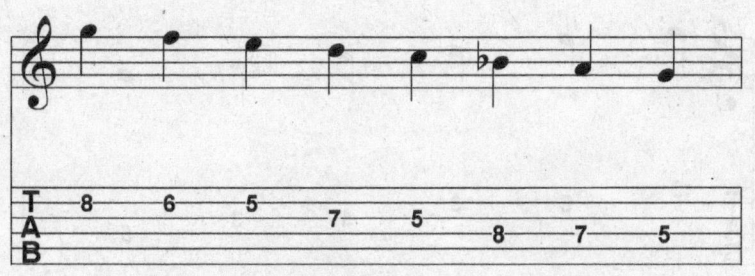

Scale pattern	G A B♭ C D E F G G F E D C B♭ A G

G
Minor Pentatonic

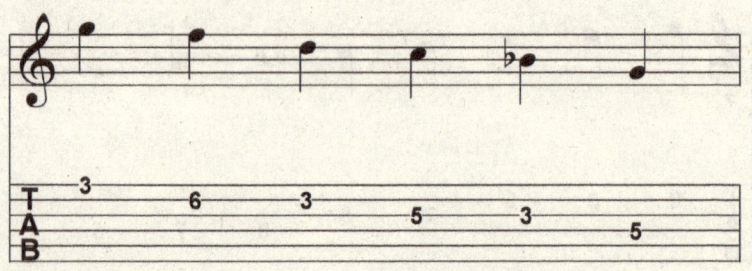

Scale pattern	G B♭ C D F G
	G F D C B♭ G

Online access
flametreemusic.com

Scan the code
to hear the chord

G
Blues

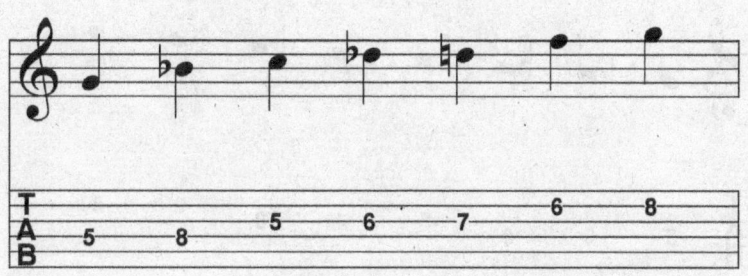

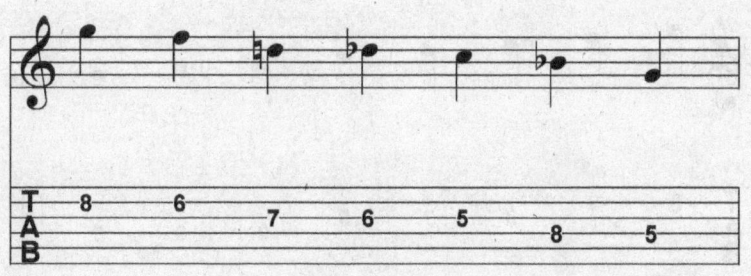

Scale pattern	G Bb C Db Dq F G
	G F Dq Db C Bb G

G
Phrygian Mode

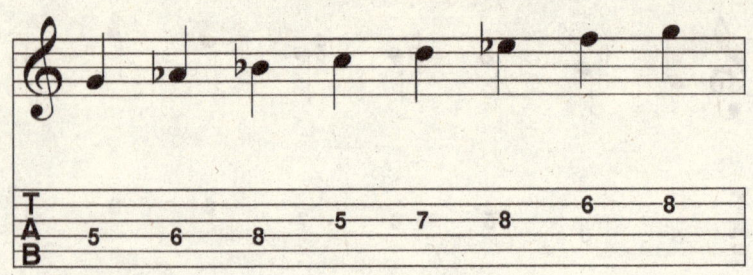

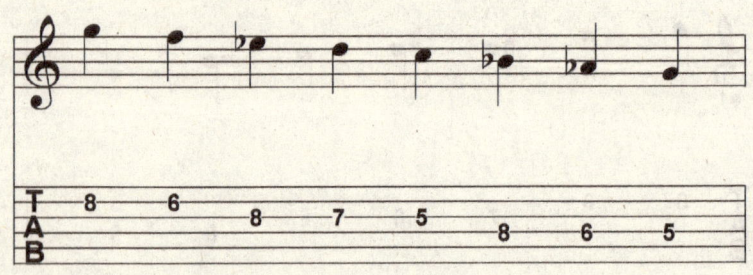

| **Scale pattern** | G A♭ B♭ C D E♭ F G |
| | G F E♭ D C B♭ A♭ G |

G
Locrian Mode

| **Scale pattern** | G A♭ B♭ C D♭ E♭ F G |
| | G F E♭ D♭ C B♭ A♭ G |

Online access
flametreemusic.com

Scan the code
to hear the chord

G
Half-diminished

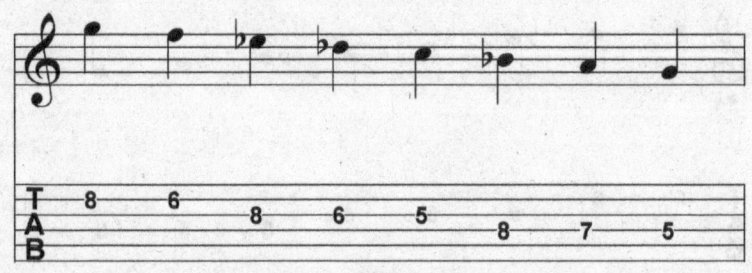

Scale pattern	G A B♭ C D♭ E♭ F G
	G F E♭ D♭ C B♭ A G

G
Mixolydian Mode

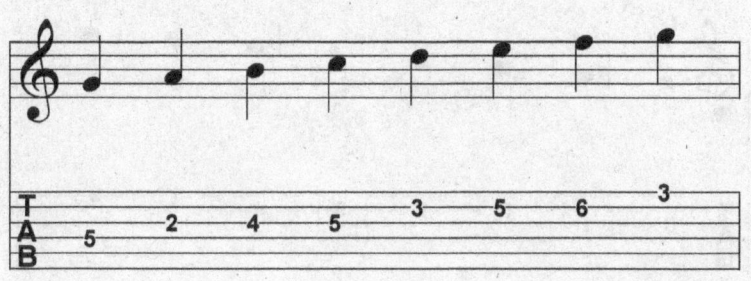

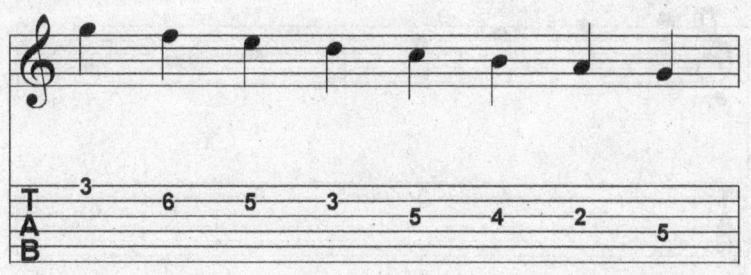

Scale pattern	G A B C D E F G
	G F E D C B A G

G
Phrygian Major/Spanish

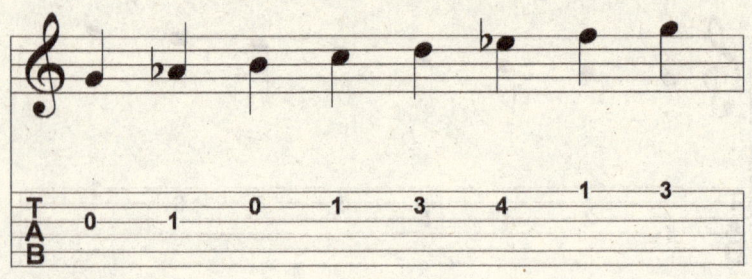

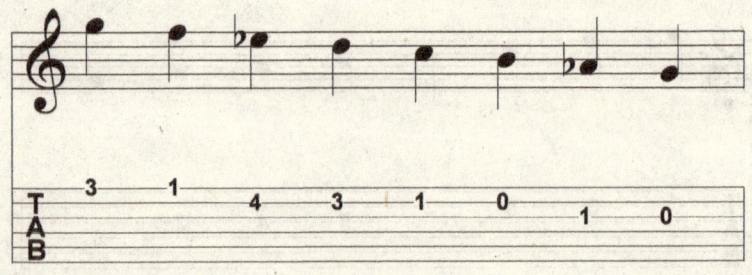

Scale pattern

G A♭ B C D E♭ F G
G F E♭ D C B A♭ G

G
Lydian Dominant

Scale pattern	G A B C♯ D E F G G F E D C♯ B A G

Online access
flametreemusic.com

Scan the code
to hear the chord

G
Diminished

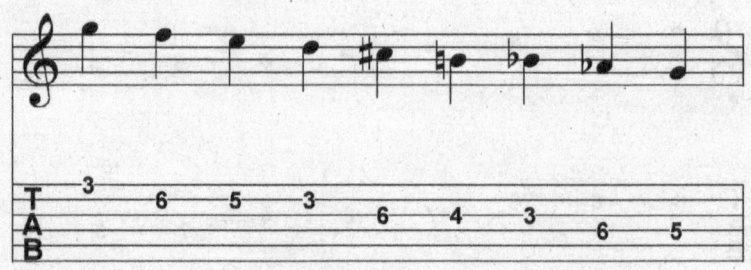

Scale pattern

G A♭ B♭ B♮ C♯ D E F G
G F E D C♯ B♮ B♭ A♭ G

G
Chromatic

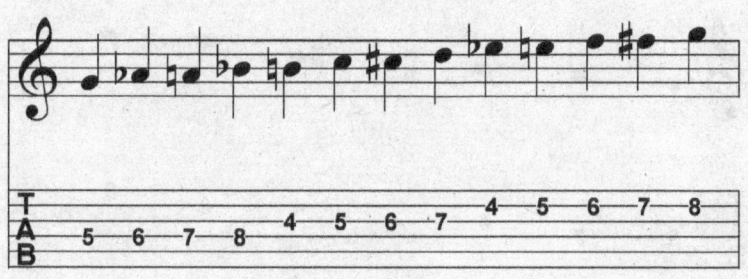

Scale pattern

G A♭ A♮ B♭ B♮ C C♯ D E♭ E♮ F F♯ G
G F♯ F♮ E E♭ D C♯ C♮ B B♭ A A♭ G

G
Wholetone

| **Scale pattern** | G A B C♯ D♯ F G |
| | G F D♯ C♯ B A G |

Online access
flametreemusic.com

Scan the code
to hear the chord

G
Neapolitan

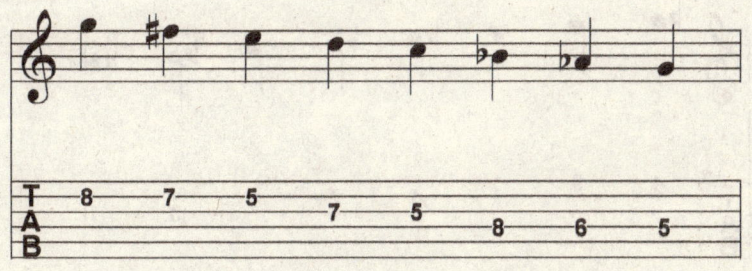

Scale pattern	G A♭ B♭ C D E F♯ G
	G F♯ E D C B♭ A♭ G

G#/A♭
Major (Ionian Mode)

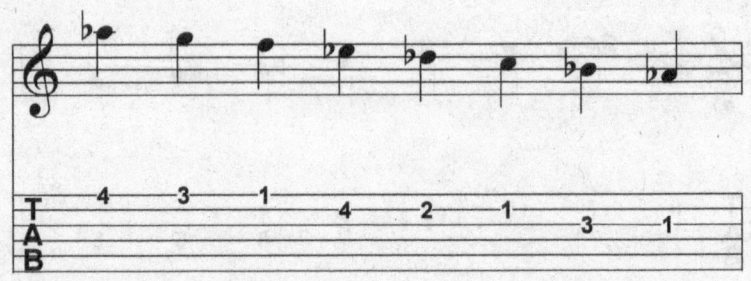

Scale pattern	A♭ B♭ C D♭ E♭ F G A♭
	A♭ G F E♭ D♭ C B♭ A♭

G♯/A♭
Major Pentatonic

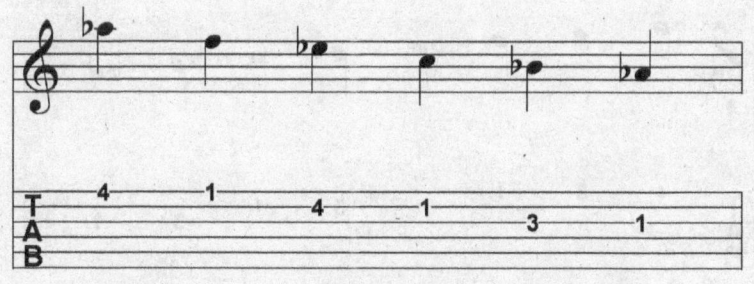

Scale pattern

A♭ B♭ C E♭ F A♭
A♭ F E♭ C B♭ A♭

G♯/A♭
Lydian Mode

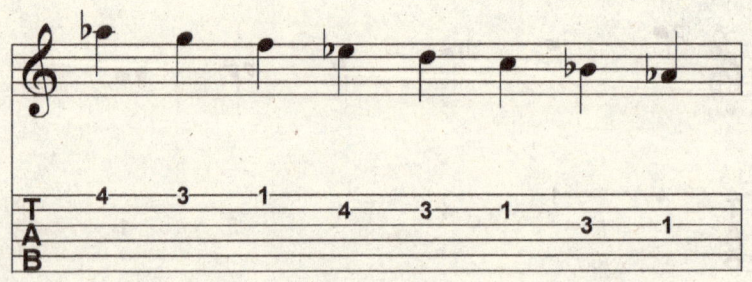

Scale pattern

A♭ B♭ C D E♭ F G A♭
A♭ G F E♭ D C B♭ A♭

G♯/A♭
Lydian Augmented

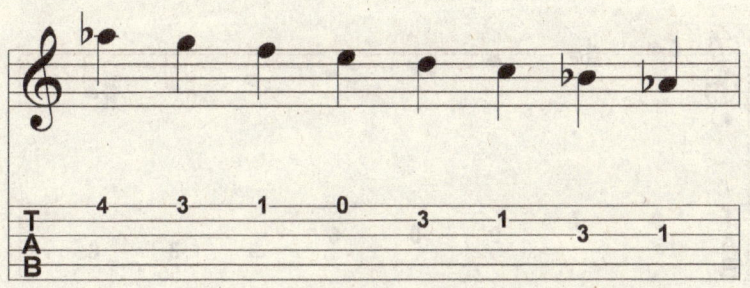

Scale pattern

A♭ B♭ C D E F G A♭
A♭ G F E D C B♭ A♭

G#/A♭
Natural Minor (Aeolian Mode)

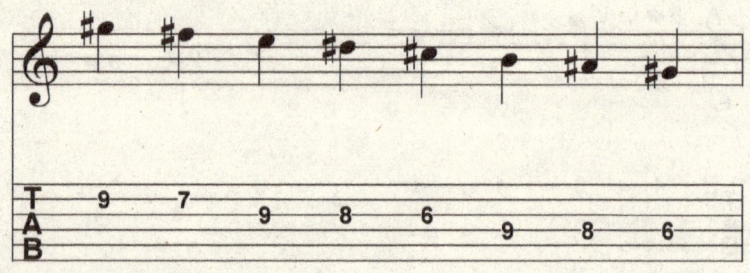

Scale pattern

G# A# B C# D# E F# G#
G# F# E D# C# B A# G#

G♯/A♭
Harmonic Minor

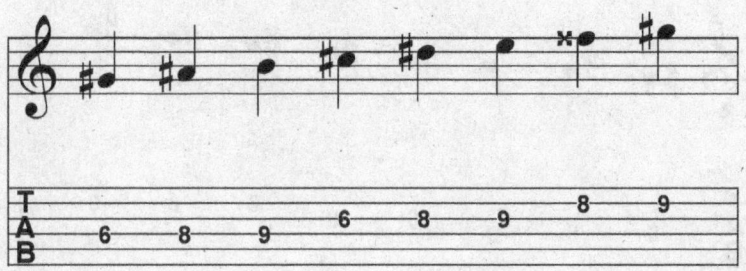

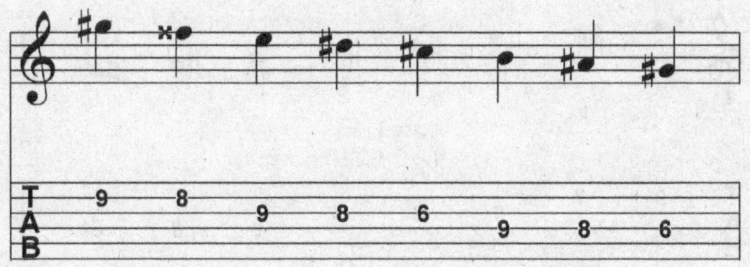

Scale pattern	G♯ A♯ B C♯ D♯ E F𝄪 G♯
	G♯ F𝄪 E D♯ C♯ B A♯ G♯

G#/A♭
Melodic Minor

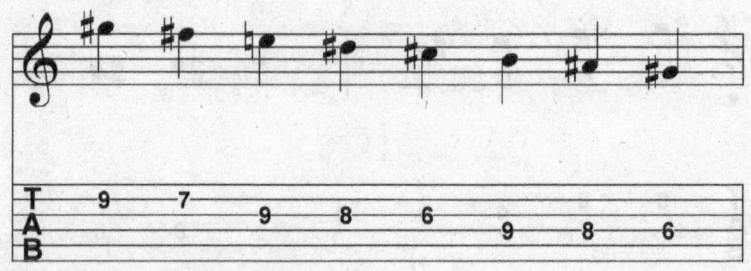

Scale pattern

G# A# B C# D# E# F× G#
G# F# E♮ D# C# B A# G#

G♯/A♭
Dorian Mode

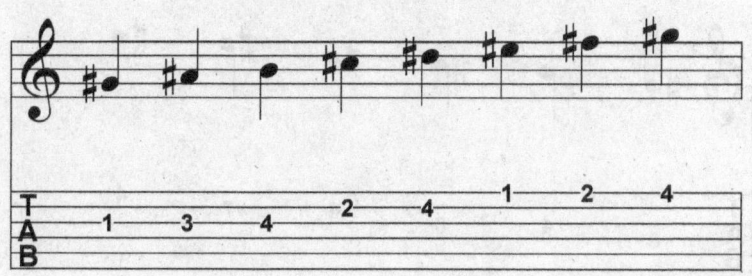

Scale pattern	G♯ A♯ B C♯ D♯ E♯ F♯ G♯
	G♯ F♯ E♯ D♯ C♯ B A♯ G♯

G#/A♭
Minor Pentatonic

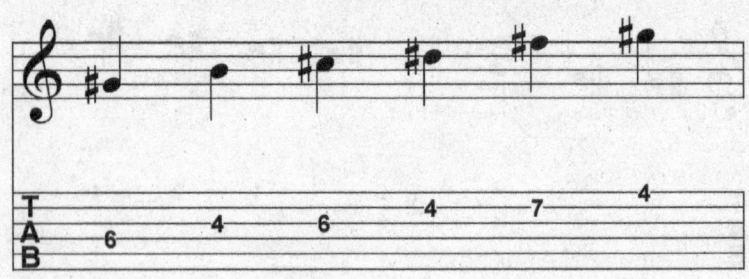

Scale pattern	G# B C# D# F# G#
	G# F# D# C# B G#

G♯/A♭
Blues

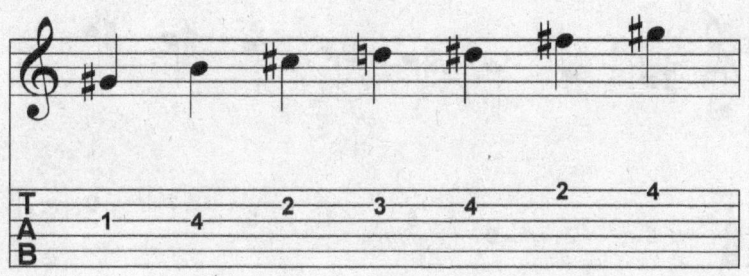

Scale pattern	G♯ B C♯ D♮ D♯ F♯ G♯
	G♯ F♯ D♯ D♮ C♯ B G♯

G♯/A♭
Phrygian Mode

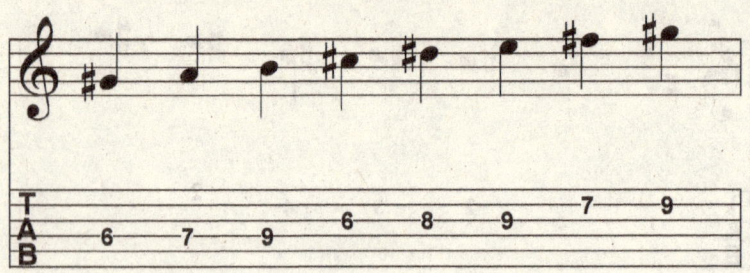

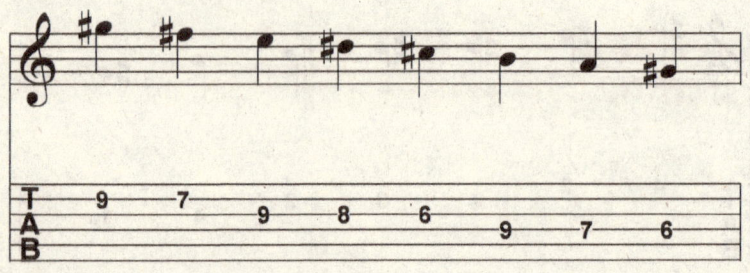

Scale pattern	G♯ A B C♯ D♯ E F♯ G♯
	G♯ F♯ E D♯ C♯ B A G♯

Online access
flametreemusic.com

Scan the code
to hear the chord

G♯/A♭
Locrian Mode

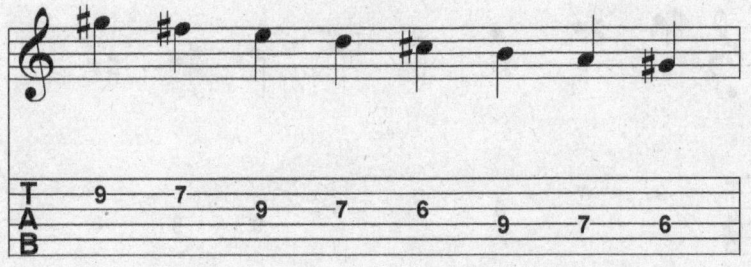

Scale pattern	G♯ A B C♯ D E F♯ G♯
	G♯ F♯ E D C♯ B A G♯

Online access
flametreemusic.com

Scan the code
to hear the chord

G#/A♭
Half-diminished

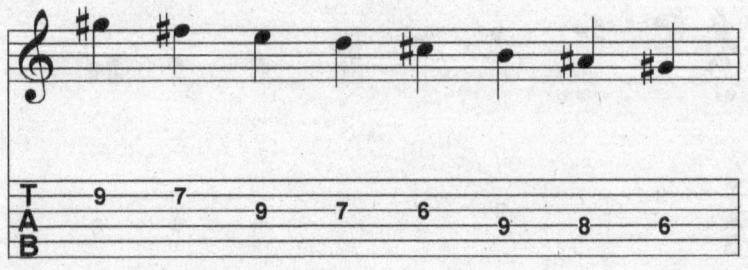

Scale pattern	G# A# B C# D E F# G#
	G# F# E D C# B A# G#

Online access
flametreemusic.com

Scan the code
to hear the chord

G#/A♭
Mixolydian Mode

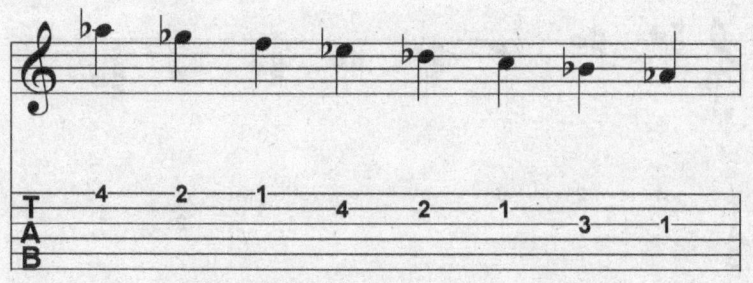

Scale pattern

A♭ B♭ C D♭ E♭ F G♭ A♭
A♭ G♭ F E♭ D♭ C B♭ A♭

Online access
flametreemusic.com

Scan the code
to hear the chord

G♯/A♭
Phrygian Major/Spanish

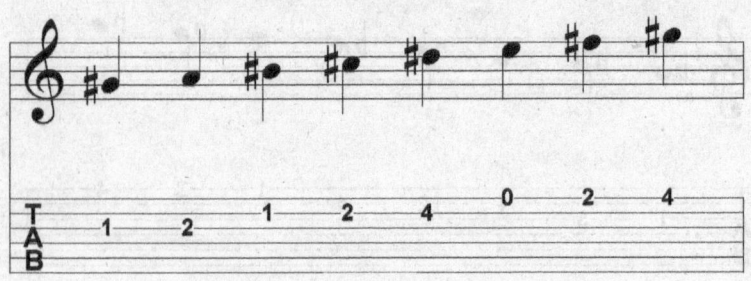

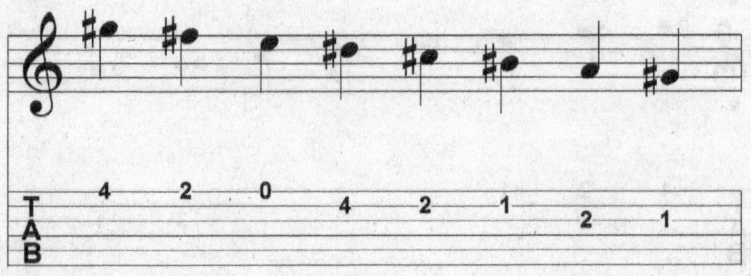

Scale pattern

G♯ A B♯ C♯ D♯ E F♯ G♯
G♯ F♯ E D♯ C♯ B♯ A G♯

G#/A♭
Lydian Dominant

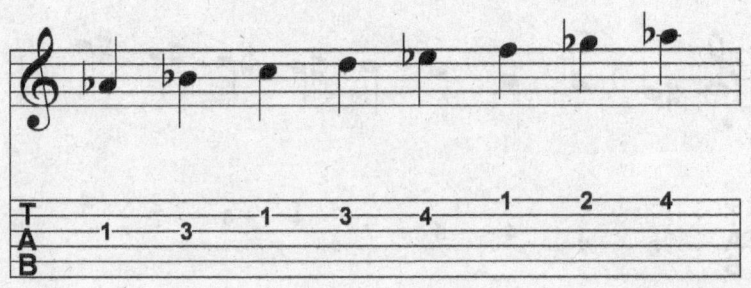

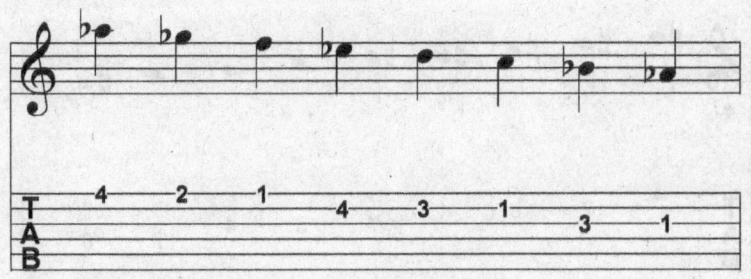

Scale pattern

A♭ B♭ C D E♭ F G♭ A♭
A♭ G♭ F E♭ D C B♭ A♭

G♯/A♭
Diminished

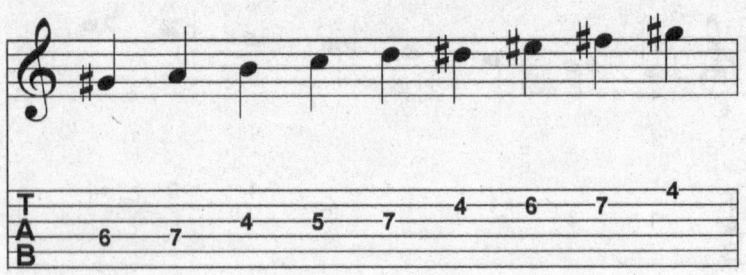

Scale pattern	G♯ A B C D D♯ E♯ F♯ G♯
	G♯ F♯ E♯ D♯ D♮ C B A G♯

Online access
flametreemusic.com

Scan the code
to hear the chord

G♯/A♭
Chromatic

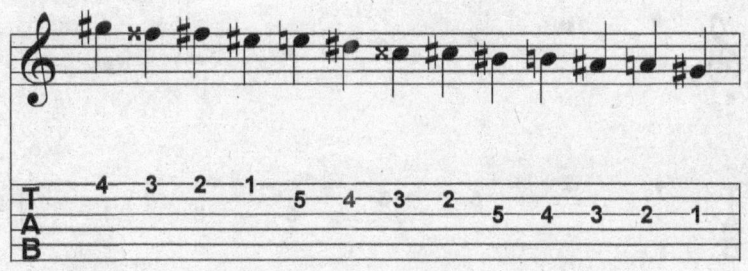

Scale pattern

| G♯ A A♯ B B♯ C♯ C✗ D♯ E E♯ F♯ F✗ G♯ |
| G♯ F✗ F♯ E♯ E♮ D♯ C✗ C♯ B♯ B♮ A♯ A♮ G♯ |

Online access
flametreemusic.com

Scan the code
to hear the chord

G♯/A♭
Wholetone

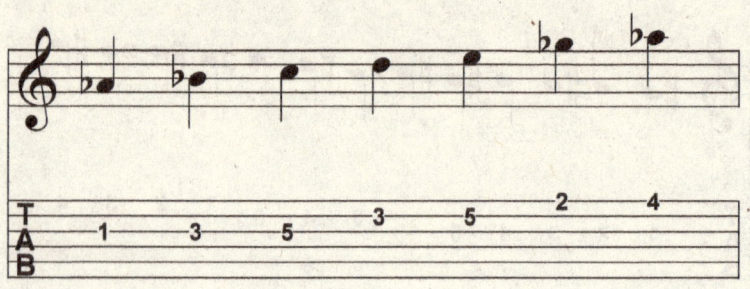

Scale pattern	A♭ B♭ C D E G♭ A♭
	A♭ G♭ E D C B♭ A♭

G♯/A♭
Neapolitan

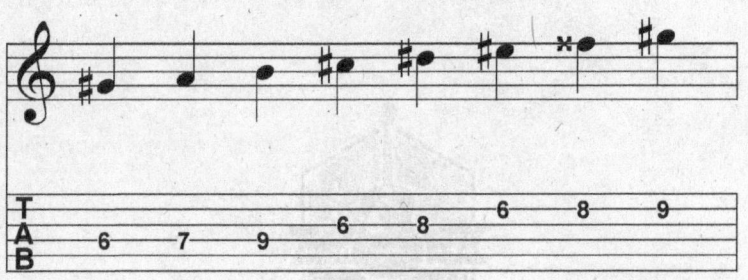

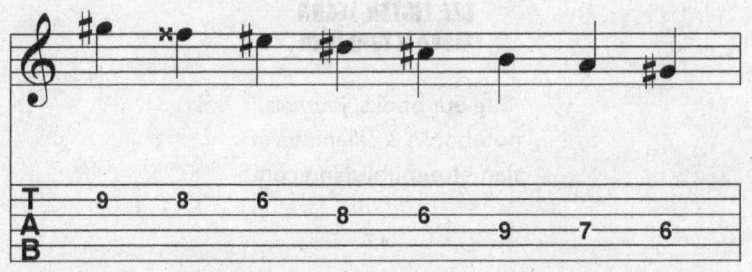

Scale pattern	G♯ A B C♯ D♯ E♯ F𝄪 G♯
	G♯ F𝄪 E♯ D♯ C♯ B A G♯

SEE, LISTEN, LEARN
Make it Your Own

See our books, journals,
notebooks & calendars at
flametreepublishing.com

•

Books in this series:
Quick Piano & Keyboard Chords
Quick Guitar Chords
Quick Left-Hand Guitar Chords
Quick Ukulele Chords
Quick How to Read Music